The Star Walk

Reflections and Records

1922 - 2000

by Malcolm Ayton

Dedication

This book is dedicated to the thousands of 'Star' Walkers throughout the years but in particular to the memory my brother Donald who died so young at the age of twenty seven but in his short life was a keen sportsman which included taking part in the 'Star' walk as a teenager and who influenced me to take the same journey; also to my sister Ann who whilst not athletically competitive took part in the 'Star' Walk for charitable causes on numerous occasions despite her worsening blindness.

Acknowledgements

This book would be much the poorer without the experience, knowledge and help of 'Star' Walk enthusiasts and I should like to thank in general Sheffield Newspapers Ltd for permission to use their copywritten material, the encouragement of Jack Bonnington and Fred Thompson who set me on the path of authorship and to Bryan Woodriff whose experience as an author helped me enormously also to the following people for their loan photographs or article contributions:- Lol Allen

Victor Bramley   John Burkhill   Ruth Crawshaw   Reg de Soysa   Adrian Good   Edwin Grocock

Anne Gurnell   Jane Hambre   Carole Hancock   Lorraine Haywood   Peter Hodgson   Val Hughes

Ann Lockwood   The Hon Austin Mitchell M.P.   Lillian Mosforth   John Shepherd jnr.

The Hon Dennis Skinner M.P.   Kelly Spurr   Audrey Trickett   Pauline Troughton

Dawn White and Jill Wilkinson.

Finally I acknowledge with gratitude the help of Sheffield Walkers administrators Brian Adams John Howley David Staniforth and in particular to Richard Holland and John Eddershaw whose expert knowledge of race walking and records is second to none.

Contents

Published by Arc Publishing and Print
166 Knowle Lane
Sheffield
S11 9SJ
Telephone 07809 172872

PREFACE

THE STAR WALK

Back in 1997 when I was Lord Mayor of Sheffield I achieved a life long ambition- no not becoming Lord Mayor- but participating in The Star Walk. Okay it was not the great challenge it once was, but the nine mile walk at speed certainly shattered me and I am the only Lord Mayor to have done the Star Walk whilst in office and at least my dad was proud of me.

I am sure all Sheffielders of my era will have fond and nostalgic memories of this great sporting event and will welcome this book. I remember after the war(I would be seven) my dad would take me every Whit Tuesday to watch the race, sometimes in town at Kemsley House (home of The Star or Kemsley Comic as my father called it), or sometimes at Barnsley Road .It was always spectacular, with crowds lining the streets, clapping and encouraging the walkers on. I am sure it must have been an inspiration to others to get their walking shoes on and have a go, just like the marathon did years later.

Sheffield has a proud sporting history, indeed in 1993 it was awarded the title of Britain's first National City of sport by Sport England and we have been the city of excellence for many sports in the U.K..
There was a time when Road Walking in Sheffield through the Sheffield United Walking club was the centre of excellence in the UK .much of it due to the influence of the Star Walk. It is such a pity this great public event was allowed to die.
I would like to thank and congratulate Malcolm Ayton for this wonderful book of reflections and records of this great race and making sure that a part of Sheffield's sporting history, the Star Walk, takes it's proper place and is not forgotten .Perhaps it may stimulate a revival, I certainly hope so, and I am sure Sport England who are trying to increase physical activity among our communities will echo that – good luck.

Councillor Peter Price MBE

Chair Sport England Yorkshire Region.

FOREWORD

In the early part of the twenty first century, Sheffield can boast of its numerous sporting facilities and activities. For example the International Institute of Sports stadium with its excellent gymnasium and indoor running track used by international athletes as well as local enthusiasts and numerous other sporting halls. There is Sheffield Don Valley Stadium where international meetings have been a regular feature over the past few years and where Olympic double gold winner Dame Kelly Holmes chose to run her final race as she closed down her long brilliant athletics career in 2005. The Ponds Forge Swimming Pool has hosted amongst other international events, the European Swimming Championships and has an area where indoor bowls attract some of the world's top bowlers in an annual tournament.

In 1991, Sheffield hosted the World Students Games and as a spin off from this event, other facilities were created for the use of local sporting people. For example the indoor and outdoor tennis courts at Norton, a newly built swimming pool at Hillsborough, outdoor floodlit hockey and football pitches at Concord Park.

Sheffield also has an ice rink where national league ice hockey matches are played. We also have the traditional football stadiums of Sheffield United and Sheffield Wednesday. World Cup matches have been played at Hillsborough. We have greyhound and speedway at the Owlerton Stadium and of course the indoor sport of snooker televised from the Crucible Theatre annually to millions of homes .

No wonder that our city is known as the City of Sport and ranks amongst the top cities in Great Britain if not in Europe for its top class facilities and events.

Historically Sheffield has a fine tradition in sport, our football teams have between them won the F.A. cup no fewer than seven occasions, although sadly not in recent years, the league cup being our sole victory in the nineties. However Sheffield has a good reputation for being involved at grass roots level ever since the mid nineteenth century when Sheffield Club was formed having a reputation as being the first ever football club in the world. Today various leagues offer teams with different standards of play. Rugby is making some headway in a city dominated by soccer. Cricket is the main summer pastime, although tennis is enjoyed as three different leagues each administering several teams.

Sheffield the Steel City has been well served in sport by the Sheffield and District Works Sports association where almost all firms are members and encourage participation in both indoor and outdoor sport. The bigger firms have their own dedicated sports premises used for leisure activities as well as sports.

Sheffield Parks also have an association which run tennis and bowls competitions and in fact Roger Taylor the Wimbledon player and one time manager of the Great Britain Davis Cup team began his tennis career at Weston Park.

This book is not however about any of the aforementioned sports but one of the less glamourous sports, a comparatively minor one if you please but major in the sense of local participation and spectating.

The sport of Race Walking gathered in the largest number of spectators in one day than any other sport. We are talking about THE 'STAR' WALK.

The Route

KEMSLEY HOUSE

The impressive white building with it's slate blue bell shaped tower on High Street now fronted by The Bradford and Bingley Building Society was previously The Star's reception office.

The dark building on the left is The National Westminster bank and the road in between the buildings is York Street where the walkers would be led out to the starting line two minutes before ten o'clock on Whit Tuesday to begin The "Star" Walk.

*The Early Dash down **SNIG HILL** to **WEST BAR**. Walkers would see old shops and not encounter the modern court building at the bottom of the hill where quarter sessions are held.*

*At **WEST BAR** the route passes the old city centre fire station now a popular fire and police museum into **SHALESMOOR** before entering Infirmary Road.*

The old Royal Infirmary, now redundant as a hospital is neatly landscaped. Here ambulances once transported patients in need of treatment but hopefully not the walkers who had at this juncture barely travelled one mile.

*In to **LANGSETT ROAD** passing the old army barracks concealing the shops and Morrison's Supermarket. It is doubtful whether the competitors would notice the areas of Wadsley and Birley Edge in the distance as they concentrated on the road ahead leading into the busy shopping centre at Hillsborough corner.*

After passing Hillsborough Park, walkers enter Leppings Lane and pass the west side of the Sheffield Wednesday football ground hidden by the foliage of the tall trees. The "next fixture" board can just be seen to the right of the end house.

The beginning of the first of three long hills and under the Wadsley railway bridge up Halifax road to **GRENOSIDE**.

So far walkers have gone through built up areas but at The **NORFOLK ARMS** *Public House a right turn in to Whitely Lane brings a different scene as pleasant countryside views are encountered.*

*The delightful hamlet of **WHITLEY** with it's old worldly charm sees a host of multi coloured vests each whit Tuesday pounding this quiet country lane. What would the blacksmith whose anvil was at the far end of this workshop in 1922 make of it?*

A quick glance to the left through the trees by the 'Star' Walkers brought a glimpse of
***THE WHITLEY HALL HOTEL**, an elegant 16th century mansion house recognised by Johannsens the leading hotel guide throughout the world and well patronised by newly weds.*

*Competitors leave Whitley Lane to join the main road from **CHAPELTOWN** to **ECCLESFIELD** opposite the popular **ARUNDEL** public house and restaurant. In the early days of the 'Star' Walk stood the cinema house.*

The corner of Whitley Lane turning right into Church Street where begins the long inward journey back to Sheffield. It was always anticipated that the leading walkers would pass the church at eleven o'clock.

11

Barnsley Road at **HARTLEY BROOK,** *the start of the second long hill to Sheffield Lane Top, on this day looking deserted but in bygone days on Whit Tuesday this road would be lined with spectators.*

The old **TOLL BAR** *house. Originally competitors turned left here down to the Wicker but a change in the course directed a right turn down Pitsmoor Road to the finish at Corporation Street.*

WICKER ARCHES *built to allow L.N.E.R line trains to pass over the road is seen in a modern setting. As competitors approached here from Spital Hill, the road on the left, they knew that the finish was less than half a mile away.*

The finish line as it was in 1955. Jack Bonnington crosses the line in first place.

Chapter One

Recollection

The first recollection I have of the "Star Walk" was in 1939 when as a young boy of eight years of age and living near Sheffield Lane Top I would follow the crowds to within a few yards from the Pheasant Inn where people gathered for a vantage point of the event.

My interest in a walking race at that time or for that matter any other sport except perhaps a game of marbles or kicking an old tennis ball around in the playground at break time was negligible.

The crowds fascinated me. Most men smoked cigarettes in those days and I was a keen cigarette card collector. Each packet of ten cigarettes contained a picture card. I would take my eyes off the race to approach these smokers and ask "Got a cigarette card mister please". I found this profitable for my collection. In retrospect, I am reminded of Charles Dickens novel Oliver Twist and the stage musical Oliver where the artful dodger goes from man to man singing "Got to pick a pocket or two".

The "Star Walk" in 1939 gave some holiday relief to the gloomy atmosphere when doubts were in people's minds as to what was happening in Europe and whether we should be involved in a war.

Three months later Great Britain was at war and it would be another six years before the next "Star Walk". As a teenager sport began to play a greater part in my life including the "Star Walk"- but more of that later.

Malcolm on the left, with younger brother Donald

Chapter Two

The Twenties - Instigation

An article in the "Yorkshire Telegraph and Star" on 1st May 1922 read :-

"STAR WALK"

Challenge Cup for Local Pedestrians - Whit Tuesday.

The proprietors of the "Yorkshire Telegraph and Star" with the object of encouraging walking as a sport have decided to give a silver trophy and other prizes for annual competition.

The first "Star Walk" will be held on Whit Tuesday June 6th.

The above announcement is sure to be read with keen interest by a number of our athletic readers. It is a sporting curiosity that although South Yorkshire and North Derbyshire contain thousands of enthusiastic ramblers and hard walkers, there is very little competitive walking in the district. Whilst other centres – London, Manchester and Bradford for instance have their great walking events every year, nothing of the kind has been held in Sheffield neighbourhood for a considerable period.

The "Yorkshire Telegraph and Star" thinks this is not as it should be, Sheffield possesses a sporting reputation second to none but great as it's programme is, there is ample room for an event which will encourage such a fine healthy pastime as road walking.

Full particulars of the "Star Walk" will be announced later on enough to say that the course will start and finish in Sheffield and will not exceed fifteen miles in all, while the event will be a scratch race as regards the chief trophy.

Our principle idea at present is to encourage the development of a number of good walkers in the district. The event will be therefore be open to all our readers permanently residing within an area of twenty miles from the "Yorkshire Telegraph and Star" offices. The only limitation apart from that is that no one will be allowed to compete who has ever won a prize for walking in competition. The "Star Walk" in short will be a scratch event for novices. Entry forms for the walk will be published in the "Star" in due course. An entrance fee of one shilling will be charged but the expenses of the event will be borne by the "Star" and all entrance fees will go to increase the prize fund. So, to encourage walking as a sport and the development of good walkers was the prime aim but later announcements gave the idea that in the early twenties only a few years after the first world war had ended social conditions were very poor, families were much larger then with 4.2 children and rising rather than recent average of 2.4 children.

There was a depression and unemployment amongst the working classes. The "Star Walk" event would bring some light hearted relief at the Whitsuntide holiday giving some "fun and sport".

Another aspect was that Whitsuntide was celebrated more in churches and chapels as one of the five most important Christian festivals, Christmas, Good Friday, Easter Day and Ascension Day being the others. Whitsuntide had a special celebration as churches and their organisations paraded from their places of worship to local parks for their annual Whit sing, this form of "walking" was hugely popular having been started around 1870 influenced by James Montgomery one time editor of the Sheffield newspaper the " Isis", preacher, social reformer and hymn writer whose large statue today stands in the Cathedral grounds only a few steps away from the "Star" offices. Whit Tuesday therefore was a good time to hold such a sporting event as the "Star Walk".

Following the original announcement on 1st May, sportsmen from many different sports applied to participate in what was now being named "The Great Star Walk", members of swimming teams, cycling clubs, footballer's and men from all walks of life were merely captivated by what appeared to be a novel event.

Such was the interest generated that 272 male entries had been received.

Two lady competitors applied to join the "Star Walk" but after consultation between the organisers and the Amateur Athletic Association it was decided to restrict the event to men and boys and in declining the ladies requests their fees were returned. It would be over fifty years before ladies were allowed to compete in the "Star Walk". A course of eleven and three quarter miles had been chosen which would start outside the newspaper's offices at High Street, proceeded down Angel street to Snig Hill and followed the tram lines to take the right hand fork at Shalesmoor, along Penistone Road. All was then plain sailing for a considerable distance beyond the Wednesday ground where a milestone says "Sheffield 2 miles". Then along the main road through Wadsley Bridge going under the bridge, and up the long hill on Halifax Road. Just beyond Parson Cross school is a sign on the opposite side of the road "To Ecclesfield" with a milestone "Penistone 10 miles, Sheffield 3miles".Competitors would keep straight ahead by the broad main road passing the low side of Grenoside and the "Red Lion" on the left until the "Norfolk Arms" is reached. There is a sign post here for Grenoside, Oughtibridge, Bradfield, Whiteley and Ecclesfield. This corner is precisely five miles from the starting place.

At the corner the route bends sharply to the right and competitors follow it through Whiteley past the charming view of Whiteley Hall all down hill - a twisty road but marked by telegraph posts. Leading into Ecclesfield and then breaking out into the big open space in front of the Cinema House (since demolished where now stands the Arundel, a public house and restaurant), one mile and 785 yards from the Norfolk Arms.

Some walkers in training took a wrong turning here where a neighbouring sign points to Sheffield. They should have taken a sharp right turn at the bottom of Whiteley Lane, here the course passes Ecclesfield Parish Church and a little further on the prominent "Black Bull" with its bold sign. The course turned left here proceeded past the Wesleyan Methodist Church and the "Ball Inn" until the road made a clear fork.

Here walkers would turn right past the bus stop sign until striking the main Sheffield road.

A long climb then ensued up to Sheffield Lane Top and the "Pheasant Inn" where the milestone indicates three miles from Sheffield. Competitors continued then in a direct line down Barnsley Road, past Fir Vale and following the tram lines uphill along Burngreave Road, Spital Hill and the Wicker over Lady's Bridge before turning right at Castle Street, up Angel Street to the finish at the point where the race commenced. A gruelling course for the initial "Star Walk", but that did not deter the novices` applications to race.

"STAR" WALK: NEW ROUTE MAP.

The above shows the route for the "Star" Walk as modified by the work on the widening of Owlerton Bridge.

The "Star" Walk route map 1923

Training had begun almost immediately following the first announcement and further notices were put out as some would be competitors lost their way when training on the proposed course particularly taking an early right turn on Halifax Road thus cutting short their training mileage. On June 1st the article in the "Star" appealed to the public to keep to the pavement leaving the road was for the walkers. Also to keep away from the starting point in order that the contestants may "have a fair field" and avoid interference with traffic. It was hoped to effect the start within two minutes of the competitors being brought out from the assembly point in York Street. The newspaper article was calling the event a tremendous success even a few days before the race was due to begin. Competitors would receive their number cards and full instructions during Whit weekend and the number cards had to be sewn prominently on walking costume and not be removed until after the event and prize giving on Tuesday afternoon. Results would not be announced until the judges and observer's reports had been received from all parts of the course.

A further article in the newspaper read :-

Competitors should note that no pace making will be allowed, followers for competitors cannot be permitted nor outside assistance such as "bottling". The proprietors had proposed to provide liquid refreshments but were advised by experts that this would do the competitors more harm than good.

Quite a different viewpoint from today's distance events particularly in half and full marathons where feeding stations are set up for the purpose of providing drinks to counteract de-hydration. No doubt some contestants, in for the fun of it, would sneak a drink perhaps from a friend along the way.

Another comment in the paper suggested that there was nothing to prevent walkers from wearing whatever clothing they wished to wear either ordinary or athletic garb but if racing costume is worn it must be adequate. The same applied to footwear either boots or shoes. This would appear to indicate various types of walkers in different clothing. Those in athletic apparel prepared for a race and those in every day clothing were out for a holiday stroll but whose ambition was nevertheless to see if they could tackle an undulating course be it in two hours five minutes or five hours two minutes.

The coveted "Star" Walk Cup

We now come to the Saturday, three days to go before the first "Star Walk". The Whitsuntide holiday period was beginning with expectations for a good time. Most competitors would be having their final training spin and many residents would be looking forward to the Whit sings and games in the park. A tradition at Whitsuntide was that children wore new clothes on Whit Sunday, at least those whose fathers were in employment. Television had not been invented and I am not sure that radio or wireless as it was known, adorned all living rooms. The cinema houses were being built but movie going was in its infancy. Films were in black and white and no sound track although the upmarket cinemas had musical organs hidden in a basement which rose up to the floor level in front of the screen. In some cinemas a pianist cleverly captured the mood of the film story with matching music. Heavy loud fast music for westerns and slow dramatic Albert Ketteleby style music for romantic scenes. The Electra cinema in Fitzalan Square, later to become the Sheffield News Theatre was showing a film called 'Carmen' starring Charlie Chaplin and described as a comedy in four parts. Smokers could buy a packet of ten Pinnace cigarettes which included a photograph of a footballer, cricketer or pugilist for eleven pence halfpenny marginally less than 5p in today's money. That's inflation for you!. A film was to be made of the "Star Walk" and shown at the Electra for three days. The following day, Sunday, was regarded as a religious day and in 1922, cinemas and other places of entertainment were closed as well as most shops. Places of worship was where people gathered and as a festival Whit Sunday was very popular. Sport was banned on Sundays so it is unlikely that walkers would be out training.

On Monday morning festive whit sings took place in Sheffield parks. Bandstands had been erected for the use of local bands which accompanied the singing. In the afternoon there were picnics, fun and games back in the park. Some walkers may have gently lumbered up for the great race on the following day.

At last the great day arrived on 6th June 1922 which thousands of people looked forward to. Competitors assembled in J J Greaves auction rooms in Aldine Court which formed part of the dressing accommodation from 9 a.m onwards. Any overflow of the huge entry changed in Hartshead Friends schoolrooms.

At 9.58 the competitors lined up in front of a stationary tram car and two minutes later at the drop of a white handkerchief by Mr H R Sleigh, the Star sports editor , the race began. Walkers from every district of Sheffield, Rotherham, Wombwell, Mexborough, Chesterfield, Elsecar, Wakefield, Thurgoland, Hemsworth and Denaby skuttled down to Shalesmoor like an army of ants before the early pacemakers began to pull away towards Hillsborough. Little is reported about that first race but the winner was H E Hoyle from Hillsborough in a time of one hour fifty three minutes which in the book of records is actually the second slowest time recorded. However considering that the walkers had had only a few weeks to prepare, it was not a bad achievement.

It had previously been announced in the "Yorkshire Telegraph and Star" that there would be twenty one prizes apart from the winner's cup which would be raced for annually. These were for the first twelve to finish, and a further eight prizes under a sealed handicap. As all walkers were classed as novices. Handicaps would be generally based on age. There was also an additional prize for the first walker to finish who was over fifty years of age.

The winner of the sealed handicap was J T Hoyle aged sixty three who was the father of the scratch winner.

There was a further article in the newspaper referring to the tremendously successful walking contest which had been carefully planned and had entailed an enormous amount of detailed work and co operation with the police. It had been a locally historic event. The walk itself had been well judged and Colonel Charles Clifford had presented the prizes. However apart from the Hoyle winners, there was no mention of other named prize winners.

Competitors line up outside the cathedral for the first "Star" Walk in 1922.

In 1923 the popularity of the event was maintained and thus establishing that the 'Star' Walk had now been firmly included in Whit Tuesday's diary pages. Some changes were made from the previous year mainly to the course. At Shalesmoor, the route turned away from Penistone Road and instead continued along Infirmary Road. Then along Langsett Road and Middlewood Road following the tram lines to Leppings Lane. Then branching off to the right almost opposite Wadsley Lane and the Park hotel towards Wadsley Bridge. At this point it joined last year's route. This extended the course to twelve miles and one hundred yards but despite this elongation, the winner was

A cartoon 1923 'DREAMING'

Harold Payne whose time was quicker than that of the previous year being one hour fifty one minutes thirty one seconds exactly one minute faster than the second placed L J Wood of Pitsmoor. The third walker was Charles Willingham only one second behind the second man home. An interesting fact is that Charles Willingham was from the same family as Ken Willingham an international footballer of the thirties who played for Huddersfield town and England and was in the famous (or was it infamous) team that played Germany in Berlin 1938 where England players reluctantly gave the German Heil Hitler salute. In 1947 Ken was working in the Sheffield steelworks and would often kick a football about with youngsters who played on the green at Heather road where Ken lived in a council house. How times have changed. Would England's number four now retire from international football then live in a council house? It is not uncommon for one member of a family to make his name in a particular sport to be followed by another member who will seek to emulate his or her achievements. The 'Star' Walk is a good example of this, many members of a family have taken part over the years.

The prizes awarded to winners were put on show in a city centre shop window and in 1923 they were as follows:-

Scratch Race: 1st "Star" cup to be held for one year and a tea set. 2nd Case of cutlery. 3rd Cake basket. 4th Rose bowl. 5th. Teapot. The 6th, 7th, 8th and 9th received large silver medals.

Sealed Handicap: 1st Case of cutlery. 2nd Cruet. 3rd Carvers. 4th Carvers. 5th and 6th Large silver medals. The 7th, 8th and 9th received small silver medals.

Special Prizes: A veterans prize for first home and one for the oldest competitor to finish the race. These were excellent mementoes for the winners but having won a prize a winner would not then be able to enter the 'Star' Walk again as he would no longer be classed as a novice.

A cartoon by Syd Beardsall appeared in the newspaper in May of a man dreaming that he had won the 'Star Walk'. This possibly captured the thoughts and dreams of every competitor.

Crowds, according to newspapers got bigger each year during the twenties and it seemed that all Sheffielders turned out to see this fascinating race and every one had a story to tell. W. Parker from Darnall, a novice won in 1924. The reporter stated that it was a plucky win by a novice who triumphed after being knocked down by a car. Apparently the judges car was beside Parker and the crowd was about four deep on either side of the road. This restricted the width of the road. Then a child ran out in front of the car causing it to brake hard and swerve catching the victor's leg with the mudguard. Thankfully only bruising was the damage and Parker was able to continue.

The accident effected the officials on the organising committee to review the course and issued a statement that as the crowds encroached on the roadway and that as conditions were different from athletic events held in an enclosed ground, they relied on the good sense of the people "not to interfere with the freedom of the pedestrians".

Possibly the main cause of interference however was the hundreds of cyclists who followed the walkers causing an impediment particularly when several walkers were bunched together.

There was no age limit then as three boys of twelve and thirteen entered and finished the course.

The Star newspaper recorded that the 'Star Walk' had the biggest entry in Britain for an A.A.A. (Amateur Athletic Association) event and on the same page a caricature of Parker was included.

In 1925 mounted police and constables who had been especially drafted in from district stations were called upon to control the ever larger crowds especially at the start and the St. John ambulance men were in attendance in case of accident. It was all well organised.

The winner was T Jones of Shiregreen, a keen sportsman who the previous year was a member of Edgar Allen football team which had won the Sheffield Works league cup.

An example of the enthusiasm to take part in the 'Star Walk' was shown by George Cook, a Barnsley miner who had to rise early to get to the start on time, no taxis then for him. The second home was an ex cathedral choir boy seventeen year old A. Darwin.

J J Mills, a furnaceman told an interesting story of how he came to enter the 'Star Walk'. He was having

An impression of the winner
W Parker in action.

a beer at his local 'pub' when his friends goaded him about his general fitness to walk and as he boasted that walking was not a problem but he could not (or would not) afford a shilling to enter. His friends then passed round a cap and collected a "bob's worth of coppers",(a shillings worth of pennies, halfpennies and farthings). So in order to save face he had no option other then to enter. He was probably one of the tail - enders and the "keep right on to the end of the road" brigade.

One competitor was disqualified for being unsuitably clothed.

In 1927 the 'Star' Walk included a team event in addition to the individual scratch and handicap prizes. Teams from Attercliffe, Brightside, Broomhall, Burngreave, Denaby, Hallam, Heeley, Hillsborough, Neepsend, Park, Rotherham, Sharrow, St Peters, St Phillips and Walkley entered and the winning team was Neepsend which included Harry Goddard, J Harrison, Alf Pickford, T Pickford, George Storer, William Weston and Leonard Wilkinson.

An odd ad appeared in the newspaper :- "It should be publicly stated that the "Star" Walk is not heavily subsidised by the shoe trade".

In the twenties other race walks began to be organised and included in athletic events. There was also a Sheffield to Rotherham walk and walking clubs were formed such as Attercliffe Walking club and Sheffield United Harriers included a walking section which was actually promoted in 1910. Many walkers joined having first become interested by the 'Star' Walk.

In 1928, eighty eight walkers lined up for the start of the race but it was pointed out to the officials that one competitor was found to be a professional sportsman and another one on the line up was recognised as a race walker who had won a prize in a previous walking race. Both entrants were disqualified and were denied taking part.

It was estimated that there were approximately six thousand spectators that had arrived in the city to see the start of the race or in the vicinity of starting area. Such was the popularity of the seventh 'Star' Walk.

The walk started at a fast pace and being bunched together, two walkers had their ankles " tapped" before reaching Snig Hill. Neither were able to continue and so hobbled back to the dressing room to collect their clothes. Another mishap occurred when a mounted policeman's horse slipped on the cobbled stoned road dismounting the policeman as he fell.

The last entry to be received before the entry closing date went astray and it was only after persuasion by the entrant that a search was made that his entry form was found in a "Gloops" box. Gloops was a children's membership club which had been formed to give interest in activities and outings and Gloops was a fictitious cat. As a result of this publicity, spectators around the course responded with "Come on Gloops you're lagging behind" etc. and caused some amusement for the crowds.

An interesting feature in the Yorkshire Telegraph and Star was a cartoon by H.Heap who had recently been employed by the newspaper to caricaturise famous dignitaries, stage and musical artistes, top sportsmen (and women) as well as local people in the news. Heap, himself was to become quite famous who captured thousands of personalities over the next thirty odd years including 'Star' Walk winners and participants. He had a lifetime interest in race walks.

Fifty seven contestants competed in 1929 and the winner for his prize won a bicycle. Perhaps not the most original prize to encourage his further development in race walking. The race was a real endurance test as the weather on Whit Tuesday was very hot and the St.John ambulance workers were needed to treat the faint hearted.

An interesting name amongst the officials for the first time was Jim Hackwood who for almost a lifetime gave himself to officiating at race walks and encouraging local enthusiasts to join Sheffield United Harriers where novices would eventually reach a high standard of fitness, style and speed.

A brief memory of the Sheffield Star Walk
by Victor Bramley

The 'Star Walk passed the top of Skinnerthorpe Road Firvale. This was the street where I lived from 1933 to 1956. I was known as Vic Oliver in those days. An old diary records me being there for this annual event on Bank Holiday Tuesday the 26th May 1952 but I watched it on more than one occasion.

This was a most popular event throughout Sheffield and the circuitous route from town and back would be lined with cheering, clapping people. Most of our street would turn out. The weather would often smile benignly but this didn't matter anyway. These were very determined participants. A downpour of rain would see them waddling along, often soaked to the skin, with their race numbers threatening to come adrift. I say 'waddling' because this word adequately described the action of some of the lesser contenders – and there were many. The more fit and serious athletes were a joy to watch as the required 'heel and toe' action set the whole body into a rather fascinating rhythm. This was before the introduction of 'trainers' and the course had to be negotiated with hard, heavy shoes, which although extremely blistering did help to swing the feet along. A part of the feet, as I understand had to be seen to be in contact with the ground at all times and this rule brought forth the classic - 'once seen never to be forgotten' movement of the body. Of course this wasn't a local invention- in fact, it was an event in the Olympic Games and there is fascinating newsreel footage of a small Italian athlete, in a state of complete exhaustion, staggering towards the finishing line, being willed (and helped) on by cloth-capped countrymen- I think maybe illegally. He certainly wasn't heel and toeing – maybe it was the marathon.

The main contenders in the"Star" Walk would appear early, whipping smartly along Firvale Bottom, elegant muscles rippling, hips swivelling and taking the formidable Barnsley Hill unflinchingly in their stride. Style was inherent in the form and aficionados of the sport took great delight in pointing out the finer points of the 'action'. As the race wore on however, the field would start to straggle and there would be plenty of 'walkers' who looked pretty exhausted and had thrown style to the wind, especially when they saw the incredibly steep hill rearing up in front of them. Sometimes they would throw away the rules altogether, show a little spirit and break into a little run, in an attempt to catch up with the ever diminishing figures on their way to Pitsmoor. It was a rough trial but many entered for it year after year and familiar figures would be recognised and given an extra cheer. Water would be offered and gladly accepted. Sometimes a figure would appear, sweating profusely past the traffic lights, bald pate shining in the sun and desperately 'hoiking' up shorts as they threatened to succumb to gravity and all the hip-swivelling that was going on. There would be some hilarious moments. Some would stop, have a laugh and a joke and then carry on. It was all taken in the best of spirits, a real family treat after a time of the intense hardship of the war.

One young aspirant and serious contender was Alfie Lowe who occasionally played for the football team that, to my credit, I had created. We called it Vale Rovers. Alfie was a very sound player and our loss was his dedication to running, being a member of one of Sheffield's athletic teams. He gave up football and spent many hours in training. I don't think he ever won the "Star Walk" but he always did very well in it. Our little group would wait for him – "Come on Alfie"!

Bill Allen wins the "Star" Walk in 1948 accompanied by the mounted policeman.

A training session for the "Star" Walk in 1947. Was the woman hoping for a clean sweep?

Chapter Three
The Thirties - Consolidation

1930 was to have been the final year that the 'Star' Walk would start and finish at High Street, and in this year standard time medals were awarded to competitors finishing in a certain time. In all, eleven medals were awarded in addition to team medals.

Changes in the course were made in 1931. The start would be at High Street and followed the previous route until the toll bar at Pitsmoor was reached. Here instead of going down Burngreave Road to the Wicker, walkers would proceed to the right of the toll bar house down Pitsmoor

Excited crowds cheer Arnold Bullock in 1931.

Road to Corporation Street where the finish was opposite the swimming baths. A hot bath was now provided for the walkers, their clothes having been put into a numbered bag and transported to the baths. Following a bath and change of clothing it was then back to Hartshead schoolrooms for a refreshing tea and prize presentation. This arrangement would continue for the next twenty nine years, a marked improvement on the previous nine years when only a hot Oxo drink was provided for finishers. The new course was eleven and half miles, half a mile or so shorter than before.

The vision of Mr H L Cooper editor of the Yorkshire Telegraph and Star, Colonel Charles Clifford whose dental hospital is a memorial to him, Mr H R Sleigh, sports editor and their 1922 colleagues was soon fulfiled as in the first ten years many race walkers who began their walking careers in the 'Star' Walk were now participating in ten and twenty mile races in both Northern and National championships. Those men who had aspirations had joined the Sheffield United Harries and Alf Pickford the 1927 winner had become a national junior champion. In the early thirties " movies" began having sound tracks and in 1932, a film of the 'Star' Walk was made by the Gaumont Sound News experts which was shown to audiences for three nights, such was the enthusiasm. A local councillor D H Foxon gave a special prize to the first walker to finish the 'Star' Walk in his Park ward which was won by Joe Curtis who finished tenth. In later years Joe was first a coach and later took part in numerous marathon runs well into his eighties and was famously known in Sheffield as Mr Marathon Man. The race winner that year was B Percival a member of Norton Woodseats local football winning team.

In 1935 Fred Woods of Bolton on Dearne finished first and was the eldest of three brothers who later emulated his feat in the thirties. J E Cross who finished third was a local boxer proving that sportsmen from widely different sports were attracted to the 'Star' Walk. Harold Woods the younger brother of Fred Woods won the event in the following year. The second man home was J Basford, a three and a half mile cross country champion with Hallamshire Harriers and in this year it was reported that at Ecclesfield, a coal merchant's lorry swerved in order to avoid contact with a competitor. On the back of

A day out for dressed up spectators at Firvale in 1938.

the vehicle was a collie dog which was thrown out on to the street, the driver being unaware of the mishap. Each year there is a story to tell, humourous or sad.May 1937 saw the coronation of King George the sixth and therefore appropriately the 'Star' Walk was known as the Coronation Walk. As a gesture a coronation supplement was issued and all walkers who finished the course were given two free tickets for reserved seats at the Regent cinema in Barkers Pool. E Marples was first man home in one hour forty six minutes, the last man came home in three hours eleven minutes. Bill Stanley, later to become a coach who trained schoolchildren was third. A visitor from London who regularly watched the London to Brighton race walk remarked that the 'Star Walk' was the best amateur athletic event he had ever watched and was quite envious that there was no comparable event in the south of England. Jack Woods the third of the brothers from Bolton on Dearne finished first in 1938, three brothers taking the trophy is a unique feat and was never repeated. The second man was Brian Steeple a member of Rotherham Harriers.

1939 saw the last of the 'Star' Walk for six years on account of the second world war and was won by H Lydon. The course this year reverted back to the earlier one of twelve miles finishing at Hartshead. The United Motor Coach Service Company offered a free seat on a tour of Derbyshire to the first fifty course finishers . In the event only forty eight men completed the course so everyone got to enjoy the trip. In addition two free cinema tickets were once again given to every finisher.

RECORDS 1922 - 1939

Year	First	Second	Third	1st Handicap	no in race
1922	H E Hoyle			J T Hoyle	272
1923	H Payne	J Wood	C Willingham	A Mitchell	
1924	W Parker	C R Hirst	G E Newbould	J Stancer	158
1925	T Jones	A Darwin	C Latimer	A Darwin	114
1926	S Grainger	A Searle	W D Yorke	R Wass	72
1927	A Pickford	J Clifford	A Beevers	H C Wilson	102
1928	R Cawthorne	C Armstrong	A Lockwood	W P Lawson	88
1929	H Snell	G Porter	P Cutts	G J Whitehouse	57
1930	C H Clay	F Streets	F Burkinshaw	T Gosling	62
1931	A Bullock	E Warrington	A Townsley	T Bacon	96
1932	B Percival	H Thorpe	W Bullock	I Tasker	66
1933	I H Bussey	R H Pickford	T Hall	A Tomlinson	55
1934	J Friel	E Clay	J W Finlay	H B Kitchen	54
1935	F Woods	H Dingle	J E Cross	C A White	48
1936	H Woods	J Basford	W Eyre	A Freeman	42
1937	E Marples	G Walton	W Stanley	A Pashley	41
1938	J Woods	B Steeple	W S Wilson	A Salvin	53
1939	H Lydon	F W Priest	G H Malpass	J Wilson	

Chapter Four
The Forties - Revival

It had been almost six long years of war and with victory in Europe in sight. The Star newspaper's directors with the help of Sheffield United Harriers walking section decided that it was time to re-commence the 'Star' Walk. Times had been hard, many men and women had enlisted in the armed forces. Others worked in ammunition factories. Many steel workers in Sheffield were working round the clock as overtime working hours becoming the normal order of the day. People were tired and by this time in May 1945 could well have become demoralised. But spirits were kept high with the end of the war in sight. Food was still in short supply and in fact rationing of food and clothing was maintained for several years after the war. Citizens wanted peace and were looking forward to a better future with normality being restored. The 'Star' Walk would at least be one of the first events to resurface. It had an entertainment value which people could equate with the old peacetime tradition at Whitsuntide for participants and spectators alike.

After planning by the organisers, Whit Tuesday was again chosen for the race and in order to encourage men in the forces to participate, the radius from Kemsley House was extended from the hitherto twenty miles to fifty miles. In the event, the cessation of hostilities in Europe ended two weeks before the race and nineteen members of the armed forces applied to enter the 'Star' Walk.

Alan Furness was the first man home. His efforts and subsequent rise in standards put him on a shortlist for the ten thousand metres event at the British Olympic Games held in London in 1948. The second man home was Edwin Grocock trained by his father who participated in the very first 'Star' Walk back in 1922. Another competitor who later became an asset to Sheffield United Walkers was Norman Hopkinson, a long distance favourite. The seventy one competitors were afterwards entertained to lunch at the British Restaurant inaugurated during the war years.

In 1946, the 'Star' Walk was called the Victory Year Event. There was a special prize for the first man home who was serving in H.M. forces and this was won by Fred Fairfax. It was estimated that two hundred thousand spectators saw the event which was won by Stanley Goodyear who had in the previous year finished in fourth position, narrowly missing the third prize which would have eliminated him from taking part in 1946. Goodyear, it was a good year for him !.

We are now approaching the golden age of race walking where novices in the 'Star' Walk went on to gain international honours. In 1947 my own interest was kindled due to a local man Raymond Howard, a police cadet who became the "bobby on the beat" arousing some enthusiasm for the event as he finished in fourth position. But the amazing fact was that the winner was twenty six years old Laurence Allen who broke the course record which had stood since 1932. 'Lol' as he was better known had had problems with his left foot as a boy and at seventeen had to wear an iron brace to correct his walking.

There are occasions when a weakness can be strenghthened by exercise, massage or other means. Correction is made and continued treatment can actually over strengthen that fault. Within a year Allen had won the ten mile Northern Road Walking Association championship, the British open ten mile championship and the Northern twenty mile championship. Quite a feat from novice to top British walker in just over twelve months. Harry Taylor was second man home followed by John Proctor who also later became a representative for his country.

The following year 1948 was also a special year for Bill Allen, older brother to Laurence who had just returned from duty in India and trained hard to reach a good standard of walking. In the race he was always behind W Grafton (who finished second) until after the eight mile mark when he caught up with the leader and at Firvale overtook to maintain a winning position until the Corporation Street finishing tape was reached.

It was estimated by those who count heads that a fantastic three hundred and fifty thousand lined the course. The mobile police as well as mounted police used a radio car to control the crowds for the first time. The late forties and fifties was the heyday of the 'Star 'Walk for spectators. 1949 saw another prolific race when Roland Hardy a Derbyshire athlete won in a new record time. His style and that of 'Lol' Allen were totally different but they both dominated middle distance walking for several years. The third placed walker was Albert Johnson who became the fourth novice within two years to rise to fame as an international walker. Les Radford won the 'Star' Walk in 1950. He was another man who overcame illness as he had bouts of rheumatism which affected his training. His standard was very good when fit but periodically he could not train for some weeks at a time.

A man in the crowd is Mr Joseph Temperton sporting a watch chain taking his eye off no 14 as he looks at the camera.

The start of the 1949 "Star" Walk and a cartoon by Heap depicting the winning trio.

Chapter Five
The Fifties - Peak Viewing

Around the time of the 1950 'Star' Walk the twenty miles British championship took place and Sheffield's two 1947 placings, 'Lol' Allen and John Proctor finished first and second.

The nineteen fifties saw Sheffield United walkers achieve the honour of being the most successful walking club in the country. Hardy and Allen represented Great Britain at Hesinki Finland in the Olympic Games as did Albert Johnson in the European Championships at Berne Switzerland. Richard Holland who participated in the 1949 'Star' Walk gained national honours at short distances and represented Yorkshire at the White City London (the home of athletics as Wembley is to football and Wimbledon to tennis) athletic meetings on numerous occasions . He was also up with Hardy and Allen at the national championships.

Roland Hardy also held the world record for ten thousand metres in 1952.

At the other extreme, the long distances of fifty kilometres had a Northern champion in Albert Johnson. Jim Hartley contested the arduous one hundred miles races and finished second in the Blackpool to Manchester and back. He covered it in eighteen hours forty eight minutes when the world record for this event was won by Vic (rolling) Stone from Earlswood in Surrey in seventeen hours twenty two minutes.

It truly is amazing that local men entering the 'Star' Walk originally for fun, or perhaps to do a self-assessment on their fitness, achieve success in this sphere of sport.

In consideration, walking is the most natural of activities. We crawl as babies and then walk for the rest of our lives. It's a daily function moving in a forward direction from where we are to our destination, placing one foot in front of the other without breaking contact with the ground beneath our feet. Race walking is the same except at speed.

Race walking became very competitive in the fifties. Novices who were keen would join Sheffield United Harriers and be given expert advice on training, and by training with the club's elite walkers, faster times in the 'Star' Walk were achieved. On three occasions in the fifties, the record was broken. In 1951 Tom Bingley won and broke Roland Hardy's record by twenty five seconds and as this was the twenty fifth annual race, called the 'Festival' Walk on account of the Festival of Britain that year. It was a good year to break the record by a second per year. The following year, the record was broken again by Bill Woodward in the closest finish yet beating Bill Merrill by just one yard. It was the first time that a television newsreel cameraman followed the race. Another quirk was that Frank Skinner an older walker was allocated the number nine and being a Sheffield Wednesday supporter requested the 'Owls' number nine shirt which was worn at that time by Derek Dooley one of Sheffield's famous sons. The request was granted and he was cheered all the way by Wednesday supporters. He won the veteran's prize.

Top Guns - Famous five of the fifties

Lol Allen, Richard Holland, and Roland Hardy.

The top five "Star" walkers who all went on to win national honours and become international representatives ensuring that Sheffield United walkers were the top team in the fifties.

Albert Johnson

John Proctor

It was in 1951 and 1952 that my personal interest in the 'Star' Walk took off. I was in the R.A.F. and stationed in Gibraltar but from home I received regular mail and my youth club at St. Hilda's entered a team in 1951 which included my brother Donald, Jack Edwards and Fred Thompson. Donald and Jack finished the race at Corporation Street but Fred was pulled out at Hillsborough for 'lifting', but Donald and Fred would try again. Donald did again in 1952 finishing sixth and won the third handicap prize. Fred entered again in 1956 and finished third.

I was determined that when I was demobilised from the R.A.F. I would have a go as did Jack Bonnington, my friend who was also a member of St. Hilda's youth club and serving in the R.A.F.

Jack Watson won the 'Star 'Walk in 1953 beating his brother in law Johnny Hinde. No records this year. In fact the slowest time since pre war and on this occasion not one veteran finished the course.

Jack became a councillor on Sheffield City Council and became the councillor responsible for the department of sport and leisure in the area thus laying good foundations for later years when the running track at Hillsborough Park was opened and other facilities for sport and leisure.

I came back to "civvy" street in January 1954 and decided to start serious training immediately for the' Star' Walk having first tried my walking ability on sports days in 1953 and entering one or two races when on leave. My general level of fitness was already quite good and I had played regularly for my unit at football.

My first experience was to join Sheffield United Harriers and got some advice on the best footwear for race walking etc.. On being taken to the club I expected a suitably designated building with changing rooms, showers and baths etc but to my dismay our 'changing rooms' was a coach on land adjacent to the Hillfoot Working Men's club, quite a let down. Perhaps I was confusing 'Sheffield United Harriers' with the football club-especially as red and white stripes was the common denominator.

I had some hard winter training. I initially found difficulty in pacing myself over four or five miles, but I settled down into a pattern of stride and speed and uplifted my mileage to ten miles. I felt quite comfortable with the pace that club members were setting in training. I trained twice a week, with the club on Wednesdays and usually on my own on Saturdays. Others were already training for the 'Star' Walk and I soon learnt who my possible adversaries were. I say adversaries but only in the sense of competition, in fact it was a very friendly club and every one got on well with each other.

George Turton seemed to be the man to watch out for, he was much quicker than me in the winter months. Jack Cavill was another but as the date for the 'Star' Walk approached, Neville Wheeler who had the experience of two previous 'Star' Walks appeared to be the biggest threat. Les Surgey also improved rapidly in the closing weeks before the event.

On the final Saturday before Whit Tuesday we had a final training spin of about seven miles and afterwards the cartoonist Heap sketched the potential winners for the 'Green 'Un' sports paper. He was usually right in his predictions.

Whit Tuesday was one of those days when people said "It never rains, always fine". But on the day in question I awoke early and yes, it was raining. After a light breakfast I set out for the changing rooms and lo and behold at two minutes to ten the sun came out. The race started at a frenetic pace and I was well back as my opponents made a dash down Angel Street as if it was a sprint. However by the time Shalesmoor was reached, several competitors had slowed down. I saw George Turton vomiting at the roadside and a few hundred yards further on I found myself in third place behind Surgey who was approximately twenty five yards in the lead. Wheeler was marginally in front of me but I soon caught up with him. This situation continued until the hill at Halifax Road and at the Parson Cross junction all three of us were walking together. At the Norfolk Arms going into Whiteley Lane, Surgey had dropped back but at the seven mile mark at Ecclesfield all three of us were together again. Entering Barnsley Road I made a determined effort to break away from the other two and at Sheffield Lane Top. I had a lead of sixty yards and was still leading when the toll bar was reached when both Wheeler and Surgey caught up with me. Wheeler took the lead and I was chasing him down the hill which knocked both of us of our normal strides as tiredness took over and legs began to wobble. At the tape in Corporation Street, the closest ever finish to the race was seen. Both Wheeler and I recorded the same time one hour thirty nine minutes twenty six seconds and Wheeler was given the verdict by a 'touch'.

It had been a marvellous experience and even if I had not been in a placed position, the enjoyment of participating in the 'Star' Walk would have been enough.

Heap did another cartoon in which he emphasised our noses. As the annual whit 'Roses' cricket match was taking place between Yorkshire and Lancashire,(the battle of the roses), he called it the "battle of the noses". Apart from the 'Star' Walk, there were other walking races in Sheffield which had been initiated as a result of the interest created by the 'Star' Walk. For some years there had been the Grimesthorpe Feast Walk, a nine miles race. Other road race walks, at that time, included a seven miles Parson Cross Community walk; a seven miles Sheffield Transport open walk; a seven miles club Boxing Day event and a seven miles Dysons Stannington walk. Additionally most big sports clubs in the area had a summer gala and sports meeting which included a two miles track walk. Likewise local miner's welfare galas also held either a track walk or open road walks including the districts of Bentley, Markham, Hickleton Main, Harworth and Bank End Barnsley.

Other race walks were entered by our local walkers at places such as Bradford, Derby and Leicester.

Three scratch race prizes and three handicap prizes were normally awarded and the 1954 to 1956 seasons saw all three 1954 leaders scooping up many prizes.

I retired from race walking in 1957 when I went back to playing tennis in summer and decided instead of playing football in winter I would take up football refereeing. Consequently I did not see Neville Wheeler for a number of years until on one occasion I was refereeing a football match when he was now managing one of the teams. The next time that we met was one extraordinary coincidence.

My family was holidaying at Grange over Sands at a Christian holiday centre. A sports day for children was organised. Neville was also on holiday with his family nearby when he saw the notice board outside his hotel advertising refreshments for day visitors at our holiday centre. I spotted him enjoying a cup of tea. We got chatting and I invited him to stay for the sports in which both our grandchildren were participating. As a novelty event we decided to have a walking race around the grounds which aroused a little amusement, only the crowds were missing. A further coincidence was that it was Whit Tuesday exactly forty four years after our big 'Star' event. Yet another coincidence our daughter Delia was a school teacher and Neville was headmaster at Intake school. One day in the assembly, when the Olympic Games were being held, Neville used the 'Star' Walk as an illustration for his topic and my daughter recognised that he was my closest competitor. He did not know her as my daughter as she used her married name.

Neville Wheeler was awarded the O.B.E. in 2006 for his services to education.

The famous 1954 race on the cobblestones at Barnsley Road

passing the ten mile marker, M. Ayton leads N. Wheeler and L.Surgey.

At the finish N. Wheeler wins by a touch or as Heap puts it "by a nose".

A replay 44 years later on playing fields at Grange over Sands.

Jack Bonnington left the R.A.F in early 1955. He and I trained together locally before he joined the Sheffield United Harriers in order to be the last of our St. Hilda's friends to

compete in the 'Star' Walk . Eight months of training reaped the rewards as Jack won the race having a big lead at the finish by about a quarter of a mile. The 'Star' Walk is normally started by the Chief Constable, the Lord Mayor or Lady Mayoress, or Editor or Sports Editor of the Star.

Jack Bonnington No1 seen here with Keith Bradford . (1955)

However on this occasion a departure from the usual routine was made when Lita Rosa, a popular singer and entertainer in the sixties, started the race after having a special cheery word for the competitors as they lined up for the start.

Jack and I encouraged and help train our friend Fred Thompson for the 1956 'Star' Walk

Fred Thompson (1956)

but due to family and church commitments his training was spasmodic. However he attained a good style and had plenty of stamina and finished third. St. Hilda's youth club was very proud of its walkers achievements.

Ken Keightley won the race and the second man home Dennis Skinner. He was a miner from a district of Chesterfield and later became a well known member of parliament who was renowned for his radical views. He had entered the 'Star' Walk to improve his fitness after giving up drinking and smoking. He was very often in the news as he worked hard for his constituents in the Bolsover ward.

Another Star walker in the 1956 event was Paddy Dowling who later developed into a long (extremely long) distance walker. At one time he was one of only two world record holders from Sheffield. The other one being the famous Sebastian Coe, now Lord Coe, in charge of the preparations for the 2012 Olympic Games in London.

The 1957 'Star' Walk was a repeat of the very first walk in 1922 and the scratch winner was Fred Winter whose father Charles Winter won the handicap race. In 1958 Derek Slinn finished first. The Sheffield University entered a team from their fuel research department which set a precedent for future teams from the 'Uni'.

Lol Allen won the twenty miles national championship in this year for the fifth time.

The record was again broken again in 1959 when Raymond Ibbotson clocked one hour

thirty four minutes forty seconds, a course record which was never to be broken. The second man was Malcolm Bingley whose time was just two seconds slower than his brother Tom the 1951 winner when he broke the course record time. Third man was a Royal Air Force officer Flight lieutenant C J Hotston from Portsmouth Athletic club who was allowed to compete as he was stationed at Doncaster.

Malcolm Ayton (1954)

Donald Ayton (1952)

RECORDS 1945 - 1949

Year	First	Second	Third		1st Handicap	no in race
1945	A Furness	E Grocock	K Naylor			71
1946	S Goodyear	H Cooke	H Batty	C Tether		78
1947	L Allen	H Taylor	J Proctor			..
1948	W Allen	W Grafton	G W Grayson	D Shaw		66
1949	R Hardy	G H Edge	A Johnson	R Watts		68

A Heap cartoon 1959.

A Heap cartoon.

Jack Bonnington   Fred Thompson   Malcolm Ayton
1955   1956   1954

A close race in 1957 pictured at Ecclesfield are

no 6 J.Eddershaw, no 17 P. Burrows and

F. Winter the eventual winner.

RECORDS 1950 - 1959

Year	First	Second	Third	1st Handicap	no in race
1950	L Radford	J Flannery	D Thomson	J Shakespeare	82
1951	T Bingley	J Hallis	T Martin	J Pym	68
1952	W Woodward	W Merrill	J Secker	G Harvey	77
1953	J Watson	J Hinde	K Haywood	A Hall	46
1954	N Wheeler	M Ayton	L Surgey	W Smith	42
1955	J Bonnington	D Shaw	K Bradford	G F Cox	54
1956	K Keighthley	D Skinner	F Thompson	F Wall	50
1957	F Winter	P Burrows	J Eddershaw	C Winter	47
1958	J D Slinn	R Johnson	M Byard	R W Varty	38
1959	R Ibbotson	M Bingley	C J Hotston	D Steeple	..

41

Chapter Six
The Sixties - Re-Routed

Comparison between the early fifties and the early sixties was significant during that ten years the social and standard of life of many had improved dramatically. Virtually full employment had given people more money to spend not only on the necessities of life, but now on 'mod cons' as well as leisure. People travelled more on holidays and it became an age when the motor car became more readily available and cost -wise within the reach of the worker. Air travel for holidays abroad was becoming more popular.

Harold MacMillan The Prime Minister uttered two slogans which summed up the atmosphere in those days when he mentioned "The wind of change" and "You've never had it so good".

It is no surprise then that the 'Star' Walk was affected due to people taking time off at Whitsuntide for a short break. Caravans being popular for a get away. By a strange paradox, crowds for the Whit Tuesday event, whilst still in evidence by large numbers, had thinned out compared with earlier years. But average entries for the 'Star' Walk in the sixties had doubled compared with the fifties.

A local wind of change began in 1960 when the course which finished at Corporation Street ended. The route was redirected from Barnsley Road at a point two hundred yards past Sheffield Lane Top to Longley Lane. Then up to Herries Road and down through the five arches to Penistone Road where walkers would turn left and into Hillsborough Park to the finish.

The twenty mile radius from Kemsley House which was the original boundary for entrants was extended and Colin Stapleford from Harby in Nottinghamshire won the event. This was the first occasion when an outsider from the Sheffield area won.

One hundred and thirty two entries in 1961 included Roy Millett who was first home. It was announced that Albert Johnson, third in 1949, had the previous day won the fifty kilometres (thirty one miles) Northern championships for the eighth successive season . Malcolm Tolley won in 1962 as did Michael Hague in 1963 when one hundred and forty six entered but only ninety five finished the course .

In 1964 the course was adjusted once more. Instead of finishing in Hillsborough Park, the walkers went on a little further to finish at the Owlerton Stadium. It was noted that some walkers from Lancashire had entered, the handicap winner C. Ellis was also an out of town competitor from Sutton in Ashfield Nottinghamshire but Michael Barker won the race.

Lady competitors were still not allowed to enter, but perhaps the day was not too far away when they would be allowed to compete. A race walk of four miles was organised by locals at the Eagle and Child Hotel Conisborough for men and ladies. This was given publicity even in The Star newspaper.

1965 saw Keith French win the 'Star' Walk at his fifth attempt. If at first you don't succeed – try, try and try again. Some men entered year after year and enjoyed the experience without ever hoping to be at the front – and there's always the handicap prizes to go for. Regulars such as John Oldfield and John Rosser from Rossington were good examples. The second home was John Grayson from the York Walking club.

The Sheffield Sporting Cavalcade took place at Owlerton Stadium in 1966 and the finish of the 'Star' Walk won by Ken Booth was a curtain raiser. The second home was a forty six year old Arthur Etches and the third Robert Larder from Wakefield. Then a heat of a beauty contest for Miss Great Britain took place followed by a football match, speedway, greyhound racing and a donkey derby in a five and a half hour spectacular. .

Of all the winners throughout the years, the most successful of all was John Warhurst who, a novice in this event went on to win a gold medal for Great Britain in the Commonwealth Games in 1974. This was an absolutely fantastic achievement, which again proves that a local event such as the 'Star' Walk can produce such a jewel in the crown. By way of contrast in 1968, a local member of parliament for Brightside, Eddie Griffiths well experienced in his own field of politics entered the 'Star' Walk but had to retire after six miles. The winner was Philip Etches the son of Arthur who was in second place two years earlier.

Jeff Ford had been in contention the previous year with John Warhurst up as far as Ecclesfield when he was disqualified for 'lifting'. He entered again in 1968 finishing in second place.

The sixties ended on a high note of entries when two hundred and forty one were received, Norman Hobson being the winner. This was the year when colourful and funny dress was worn. For example one man was wearing a pair of pyjamas and one draped in a Union Jack flag.

Records 1960 - 1969.

Year	First	Second	Third	1st Handicap	no in race
1960C	Stapleford	J Taylor	M Grace	H Kaye	85
1961	R Millett	R Jackson	J M Ireland	A J Shelton	88
1962	M Tolley	C Redman	T Marlowe	G Barrows	130
1963	M Hague	B Johnson	D White	P Farrell	146
1964	M Barker	V Hague	J Tyree	C Ellis	103
1965	K French	J Grayson	B Mawer	M P Casey	123
1966	K Booth	A Etches	R Larder	D Learad	154
1967	J Warhurst	J Hinds	J Goodman	G Wood	202
1968	P Etches	J Ford	T Edley	J Burns	222
1969	N Hobson	C Cardwell	L Pedrye		241

Chapter Seven
The Seventies - Sexual Equality

The nineteen seventies saw numerous changes affecting the 'Star' Walk. If the sixties saw the wind of change then it could be said that the seventies would experience the whirlwind of change.

First there was a change in the calendar as Spring Bank Holiday was instituted as a fixed holiday whereas the Whitsuntide holiday was moveable between mid May and mid June . Secondly there was a change in the 'Star' Walk course.

Thirdly, a new breed of novice walkers at the minimum age of sixteen were taking part – and winning.

Fourthly, a separate race for women was inaugurated during this period and fifthly an emphasis on sponsorship as walkers were encouraged to collect monies for their favourite charities. All this resulted in an explosion of entries for the 'Star' Walk year upon year.

In 1970, two hundred and two walkers started the race resulting in a win for T.Bardsley who hailed from Failsworth near Oldham. Keith Hardwick, who was in with a chance collapsed on Herries Road not too far from the finish and was taken to hospital where he later recovered from exhaustion. The M.P. Dennis Skinner travelled on his bicycle to watch a local constituent P. Chapman, from Newbould, who finished in third position. The course had been altered again so that the finish was in Hillsborough Park. As well as the 'Star' Walk on that day, sporting enthusiasts had their minds on the England football team who were in New Mexico City for the World Cup as news filtered through that the England captain Bobbie Moore had been arrested and detained in Bogota Columbia, for allegedly stealing a bracelet. He was later released without charge.

A record to date, although soon to be broken was that the entries in 1971 passed the three hundred mark . People from all walks of life (excuse the pun) entered including nurses, doctors, local and national politicians etc. One famous T.V. personality Austin Mitchell took part and Yorkshire Television were filming the event. Austin, after several miles, cadged a lift on the back of the cameraman's vehicle and was promptly disqualified. Fancy dress costumes were worn by those whose idea of a day out was a carnival, similar to Sheffield University's rag day or the Lord Mayor's parade. Serious walkers however were evident and the winner was T Stevenson.

In 1972 , the 'Star' Walk having been going since 1922 celebrated it's Golden Jubilee when three hundred and sixty five novices entered the event. The youngest ever winner was a sixteen year old schoolboy Paul Slinn whose father won the event in 1958 and trained Paul. One of the guests at this Jubilee was Cyril Coulson who in the very first 'Star' Walk finished in forty first position. He continued hard training and took part in the 1924 Olympic Games.

Cyril is now a retired Bradford City police officer and was five times National police champion.

Seventeen police cadets entered and were sponsored for the Star's newspaper charity. Austin Mitchell decided not to take part, but said that he would sponsor the last person home. This showed great sportsmanship.

Bill Stanley was a little man with a big heart. He entered the 'Star' Walk in 1937 and came in third. After the war ended in 1945 he trained with Sheffield United Harriers and later became a coach . He particularly specialised in training the younger members and believed that training should be fun as well as instilling discipline . It was whilst he was caretaker at Newfield Green school that he had an input into the school's cross country teams and with the co operation from the teachers, he was given the freedom to coach schoolchildren. This brought them into the world of race walking which at that time was alien to children in that area.

His work came into fruition in 1973 when he coached a young boy called Barry Lines, and entered him for the' Star' Walk. Barry won, and during the next four years, still classed as a junior, became the winner of the All England schoolboy championships, and the United Kingdom record holder for the junior three thousand metres, the 1975 senior Yorkshire three thousand metres champion and the National Youth Champion. He represented England against Sweden and West Germany. David Staniforth who was second was also one of Bill's boys.

Bill Stanley's juniors were known as the Newfield Roadhogs and he produced another good walker in sixteen year old Gary MacDonald, winner of the 1975 'Star Walk'.

The emphasis on youth was paying dividends as sixteen year olds were praised for their participation and completing eleven or twelve miles. In earlier years it was never envisaged that such young boys would ever match novices of older years.

To put matters in perspective however, an occasional golden oldie belies his years by beating younger opponents. Such a participant was a fifty four year old John Johns of Doncaster who finished in fourth position.

Arnold Woodruff, a Customs and Excise official who had kept pace with MacDonald and led for quite some time was overcome by exhaustion a mile from home and had to be transported back to the stadium where he recovered. He would attempt the event again in 1976 where again he was in contention for first place but slowed down and had to be content with second place.

In 1974 R Siddall won the 'Star' Walk and the spectators who had crowded the starting point, began to sing "You'll never walk alone".

A limited number of three hundred and fifty entries was imposed in 1976 and Ray Hankin, who was tenth the previous year, finished in first place.

Corporal Douglas Voyse of Intake did some army training in the 'Star' Walk by carrying a twenty two pounds pack on his back. Men enter for all sorts of reasons.

A restricted four hundred men were permitted to enter in 1977 but two of the number turned out to be gate crashing women who managed to pass the entry system by having bisexual names such as Jackie! They were found out at the starting line up and told that Amateur Athletic Association rules forbade mixed races . The ladies in question however had several sponsors for a charity and in order not to disappoint their benefactors, they waited until the men had disappeared from the starting line, and then walked around the course to be greeted by a rousing reception in Hillsborough Park.

Cyril Haywood led home the three hundred and seventy eight finishers at his fifth attempt.

David Staniforth a successful competitor, his interest began at

Newfield Green school.

Bill Stanleys Boys Teams

Bill Stanley's Newfield Green Team 1. Barry Lines on the extreme left.

Bill Stanley's Newfield Green Team 2.

An exhausted Terry Stevenson after his win in 1971 at Owlerton Stadium is upheld by officials Messrs

Eddershaw and Hopkinson as a St. John ambulance man in attendance comes to his aid.

A group of walkers in the 1976 event on their way to Hillsborough. No. 137 is Trevor 'Sid' Greatbach.

It was decided in 1978 to allow women to compete in the 'Star' Walk but it had to be a separate race from the men. The men would tread the normal course but the women would start their race from the Sheffield Wednesday football stadium and pick up the same course as the men from this point, giving them a total mileage of nine miles.

Interest and enthusiasm was at its' peak and a staggering total of five hundred and forty men and one hundred and fifty three women were allowed to compete. Terence Kent won the race but Barry Mosley who was in second place at the five arches in Herries Road collapsed through exhaustion and was taken to hospital where he was detained for observation.

It was becoming quite a habit, men in leading positions collapsing in the final stages of a race.

The leading lady of this initial race for women was Jill Clarke, a second year student at Birmingham University but also a member of Sheffield Athletic Club as a runner.

Barry Mosley recovered from his misfortune in 1978 and returned for more punishment in 1979. Once again he was up with the leader Sam Tonks at Sheffield Lane Top when he was taken ill and had to withdraw. The race was started by three wheelchair marathon heroes and once again record entries were received, five hundred and seventy three men and one hundred and seventy six women. Jane Furniss was the first lady home followed by two sisters Janice Marsden and Karen Finney.

Lilian Hamre finds a walking companion on Herries Road

in the initial ladies 'Star' Walk in 1978.

RECORDS 1970 to 1979

Year	First	Second	Third	no in race
1970	T Bardsley	A Mulcrone	P Chapman	202
1971	T Stevenson	R Fox	R Chafer	306
1972	P Slinn	T Hartson	J Cheetham	365
1973	B Lines	Stainforth	G Marriott	250
1974	R Siddall	M Greasley	A Wicker	224
1975	G MacDonald	C Suter	T Carroll	222
1976	R Hankin	A Woodruff	I Wainwright	350
1977	C Haywood	B Bolton	S Lemon	400
1978	T Kent	J Atterton	J Root	542
1979	S Tonks	C Master	A Whitehead	573

Some 'Star' Walk Winners

Cyril Haywood, Hillsborough Park finish (1977).

Elaine Allen no 15 (1982).

Bill Woodward No 83 (1952)
seen here with Richard Holland
and Alfie Lowe.

Les Radford No 64 (1950)
Picture not taken in Sheffield.

Les Morton No 14 with Gary Crossland
finishing together in 1983.

Neil Simpson and Lorna Lancaster 1991 winners.

51

SAM TONKS
STAR WALK
WINNER
1979

Sam Tonks (1979)

Sam with Tom Bingley winner in 1951.

The final twenty years of the twentieth century saw a dramatic change in the nature of the 'Star' Walk.

At the beginning of the eighties, race walking had a rival which became very popular – the marathon. Christopher Brasher one time Olympic steeplechase gold medal winner, had an idea which developed into the London Marathon and caught the imagination of the British public. This was partly because it was televised and, in no time at all men and women of all ages began jogging and entering into fun runs. This phenomenon had an effect on the 'Star' Walk in different ways . Sheffield and Rotherham along with other cities and towns started their own marathons or half marathons and the craze for running was such that thousands of people participated. Crowds liked to watch runners especially as fun runners would dress up in various attire and collect for their favourite charities. There is no doubt that people were influenced by friends taking part in fun runs but the 'Star' Walk had an alternative exercise as those who could not run could at least walk and this boosted the number of entries for the 'Star' Walk. There was a dramatic increase in entries which peaked at seven hundred and ninety two men and five hundred and sixty nine women by the mid eighties. Thereafter the number of entries decreased just as it had dramatically earlier increased .

Whilst at it's peak boys and girls were also encouraged to do more exercise and the 'Star' Walk was again extended to allow juniors to compete in a separate race.

The minimum age to compete was sixteen years of age but the extra competitive walks allowed children to enter a three mile race, later changed to three thousand metres. This developed into junior sections of separate races for boys and girls from between thirteen to sixteen years of age. There was also a race for under thirteens.

There was no restriction on juniors winning prizes each year thus enabling winners to participate in succeeding years whilst still being classed as junior novices.

Emphasis was also made on team entries to foster team spirit.

In earlier days when entries numbered less than one hundred, the 'Star' Walk was almost exclusively competitive. A dozen or so walkers would average around six miles per hour and the winner average seven miles per hour, which was recognised by The Race Walking Association as first class.

As numbers increased to several hundred, race times changed significantly and on one occasion the winner's time was just under two hours. The main reason for this is that the majority of walkers entered for the carnival atmosphere which had developed and for the purpose of collecting monies for charities.

Vicky Lupton with the ladies rose bowl.

A young Craig Wilkinson with some Blades supporters.

Craig Wilkinson centre celebrates his victory with Hugh O'Mara left and Mark Hall.

RECORDS

Women 1978 To 1989

Year	1st	2nd	3rd	no in race
1978	Jill Clarke	Marlene Wicken	Helen Glossop	153
1979	Jane Furness	Janis Marsden	Karen Finney	176
1980	Brenda Lupton	Diane Wood	Carol Bark	131
1981	Helen Elleker	Jean Stockdale	Barbara Ashworth	253
1982	Elaine Allen	Wendy Brooks	Marian Harris	300
1983	Patricia Hodgkinson	Juliet Francis	June Boylan	424
1984	Kay Woodruff	Vicky Drury	Jill Wilkinson	569
1985	Christine Jackson	Sandra Thompson	Dawn Buxton	555
1986	Betty Sworowski	Susan Gibson	Jean James	518
1987	Louise Carr	Sue Parr	Jaqueline Bennett	338
1988	Victoria Lupton	Zena Lindley	Sarah Thompson	375
1989	Zena Lindley	Janice Carrier	Diane O'Kane	371

Men 1980 to 1989

Year	1st	2nd	3rd	no in race
1980	Bill Dean	David Masters	Chris Bolton	568
1981	Steve Dawson	Daren Morley	Derek Hurditch	600
1982	Trevor Dickinson	Gary Turley	George Crossland	571
1983	Les Morton Gary Crossland		Ken Rowe	792
1984	Trevor Hibberd	Neil Pearson	Melvin Beaver	760
1985	Tony Wright	Melvin Rawson	Derrick Stancliffe	662
1986	Russell Shimwell	Tony Keddie	Mark Ward	583
1987	Kevin Hatton	John Lindley	Gerald Barlow	411
1988	Don Longley	Richard Harris	Stephen Hill	329
1989	Craig Wilkinson	Mark Hall	Hugh O'Mara	367

Juniors 1985 to 1989

Year		1st	2nd	3rd	no in race
1985		Susan Ashforth	Joanne Ashforth	Matthew Hodgkinson	250
1986		Leigh Devlin	Tracey Devlin	Joanne Ashforth	250
1987		Steven White	Ian Jowitt	Tracey Devlin	181
1988	girls	Tracey Devlin	Zena Lindley	Sarah Thompson	
1988	boys	Stephen White	Neil Simpson	Robert Watson	141
1989	girls	Amanda Gould	Lucie Butterley	Marie Walker	
1989	boys	Neil Simpson	Robert Hall	Robert England	145

Chapter Eight
The Eighties - Peak Participation

We saw how Barry Mosley, up in front in 1978, collapsed and the following year retired ill. In 1980 he made a third attempt to win the 'Star' Walk and he did cross the finishing line before his competitors. However it was third time unlucky as he was later disqualified. Three judges at different sections of the course adjudged him to be 'lifting'. That is not heal and toe walking. The winner was Bill Dean. Brenda Lupton won the ladies event. She was the mother of three children and would later represent her country as an athlete. Roger Moffatt, a well known Radio Hallam disc jockey was a popular competitor. One of the 'Star' Walk officials, Brian Adams originally raced for the Leicester Walking club. He is now a teacher in Sheffield and a member of The Sheffield United Harriers. He took part in the Montreal Olympics in 1976 and was still one of the country's leading walkers. He turned down the opportunity to go to the Moscow Olympics in a protest against the persecution of Christians in The Soviet Union at that time.

Steve Dawson and Helen Elleker won their respective races in 1981. The three leading ladies included Jean Stockdale and Barbara Ashworth. They all represented The Crown at Totley. A few days before the 'Star' Walk in 1982, the Sheffield Marathon attracted four thousand five hundred runners but this did not deter a good turn out for the 'Star' Walk . Two brothers George and Gary Crossland were amongst the favourites to win but Gary collapsed outside the Sheffield Wednesday football ground leaving forty six year old Trevor Dickinson to win. George Crossland finished in third position.

The ladies race was won by Elaine Allen. (The daughter of 'Lol' one time winner who also represented Great Britain at the 1950 European Championships and 1952 Olympics.) At the start of the race as five hundred and seventy one men gathered, a stampede developed at the starter's signal and the chief official Jim Hackwood, who was eighty five years of age, was injured by the surge and suffered cuts to his head and hands. Fortunately Jim recovered to resume his favourite pastime.

The emphasis this year was on sponsorship and two prizes were at stake for the collector of the most money for charities. A prize presentation following the race and special gala night was introduced for this purpose.

In 1983 (seventy-eight years after the first walk) the highest number of male competitors took part - seven hundred and ninety two. This was followed in 1984 by the highest combined number of men and women competitors - in total one thousand, three hundred and twenty nine.

1983 was special in that two competitors Les Morton and Gary Crossland who had collapsed the previous year contrived a result. Nearing the finish of the race with both competitors vying for first place, they both decided to put their arms around each other's shoulders to cross the finishing line together thus ensuring the first ever dead-heat.

Such friendliness was not seen in the fifties when on two occasions races were very close and the competitive spirit prevailed. Nevertheless friendships developed and there was never any aggravation after a race. Patricia Hodgkinson finished first in the ladies event. In 1984 children were allowed to compete in their own 'Star' Walk for the first time but in a separate race which started at High Street and finished approximately three miles away in Hillsborough Park.

In the men's race the first three home were Trevor Hibberd, Mark Wall and Neil Pearson. However later it was discovered that Mark Wall had won a prize in Scotland only the previous week and was consequently disqualified. Melvin Beaver, who had finished in fourth position, was then given the third prize.

Kay Woodruff won the ladies first prize.

Numbers of entries began to decline from the mid eighties. Gradually at first, but in 1988 and the four succeeding years, women's entries outnumbered those of the men.

A special sponsorship began in 1989 following the worst ever sporting disaster to occur in Sheffield and a black day for sports loving people everywhere. On the fifteenth of April 1989 ninety six people lost their lives at the Sheffield Wednesday football ground during a F.A. cup semi-final between Liverpool and Nottingham Forest. The main Leppings Lane gates were opened to alleviate crushing but this caused a sudden rush of spectators entering through a tunnel. This made for further crushing in the ground and the compacting of people at

The Hillsborough football disaster MEMORIAL outside the Sheffield Wednesday football ground. Several walkers from Liverpool and Nottingham competed in the 'Star' Walk to boost funds for the disaster appeal. Three 'Owls' supporters, Dennis Burgin, Harry Moore and Frank Marson pay their own tribute.

the front who had no means of escape. A special fund was set up mainly for relatives of the dead – the Hillsborough Disaster Fund. Special dispensation was given to people living in the two relevant cities to take part in the 'Star' Walk and forty people from Liverpool including Chris Oakley, editor of the Liverpool Echo. The editor of the Star, Michael Corney also entered the event which boosted funds for the appeal.

In 1991 Savacentre, the supermarket stores, sponsored the 'Star' Walk. For the first time the course for both men and women was twelve miles. The women's race had been extended by three miles. The following year drinking stations along the route were introduced, drinks being provided by the sponsor.

The traditional day of the' Star' Walk had always been Tuesday but in 1992 it was changed to Spring Bank Holiday Monday as the Tuesday was no longer a Bank Holiday. Savacentre sponsored again in 1993 and gave a prize of one hundred pound's worth of their shop vouchers to the winner who was Alan Thompson.

John Burkhill a well known pram pusher in the 'Star' Walk celebrated his twentieth year in the event and estimated that he had collected between twenty and thirty thousand pounds during that time for charitable causes.

The alteration from a Monday to a Tuesday was not exactly a success and with holiday traffic becoming heavier each year, it was decided in 1994 to have the 'Star' Walk on a Sunday. In order to reduce city traffic the course was reduced to nine miles which would commence and finish at the City Police Niagara sports ground at Clay Wheels Lane. The route would pick up Penistone Road North to Halifax Road and continue as before finishing via Herries Road into Claywheels Lane.

In an increasing world of sexual equality, Nina Howley dealt a major blow to men's pride and enhanced the competitive spirit for women by becoming the first competitor home. The only woman ever to have held the coveted 'Star' Walk trophy for a year.

Two more cups introduced, one for the ladies event and the other for the overall winner.

Pauline Troughton is proud of her mum in the 1984 event.

Reg De Soysa entered the 'Star' Walk many times.

Some of Reg's friends enjoy the event.

The 'Star' centenary cloth badge was proudly worn by Reg

A selection of serious and fun walkers in 1986 climb the steep slope to Sheffield Lane top.

(pictures by Ted Mosforth)

Chapter Nine
The Nineties - Decline

The emphasis on taking part in the 'Star' Walk in 1995, was on fun and collecting money for charities. However there were still walkers who trained competitively and wanted to win the event. This was proved by the Oldale brothers, Richard and Robert who finished first and second respectively and within a year Richard represented his country in a four nations race walking championship at Moscow. But our total number of competitors was down to one hundred and fifty.

The decline was now inevitable and even in the Star newspaper, the race which had for nearly seventy years been reported on the first page was now relegated to page eleven. Prizes for the winners were now presented on the same day at the Niagara ground. The competitors number cards this year carried a slogan "Do you carry your donor card?"

In 1996 the event was called "The Star Walk for Charity", implying the object of the exercise. Sheffield City Councillor, Peter Price, who had been a leading personality in the organisation of the World Student Games in 1991 and the managing director of Sheffield Newspapers Ltd, David Edmundson took part in order to lend weight to the event. Competitively it was a family affair. Robert Oldale was the men's winner, his wife Wendy the women's winner and to complete a family hat trick Lianne won the under eleven's race. Schoolchildren were being encouraged to take part in walking races. In 1997, a local firm, J Ford Welding Services sponsored the event and a prize of five hundred pounds was awarded to the school which entered the most pupils.

In 1998 a prize of one thousand pounds was put up for an inter schools competition called "The race for life challenge". The winning school was Meadowhead led by Nathan Adams who won the boys race, the school using the money for a computer and ancillary equipment.

It is interesting to note that in the year 1999 the oldest competitor was John Shepherd from Shiregreen whose life span covered the entire years that the 'Star' Walk had taken place. John was the last active competitor to finish as an octogenarian.

Sadly the final 'Star' Walk was held in 2000 as part of "the Mayfest" held in Hillsborough Park. The nature of the event had changed dramatically over the years and what had become an institution in Sheffield was no more.

The decline in public spectating, the amount of modern traffic on the course which, allied to safety on the highways meant that the police personnel needed to effectively control traffic was disproportionate to the number of competitors involved. The cost of policing, which may have included a fair amount of overtime working, was unjustifiable as far as the organisers were concerned.

The Lord Mayor Councillor Peter Price with David Edmundson, managing director of Sheffield Newspapers at Sheffield Lane Top. Once, large crowds gathered here but we now see a near deserted Barnsley Road.

Winners' presentation 1991.

Winners' presentation 1990.

61

Many of the people who had entered the 'Star' Walk for several years, collecting for their charities were extremely disappointed when in the new millennium the walks had come to an end.

There would always be the marathon but as the saying goes :-

"You've got to learn to walk before you can run".

It was a great disappointment that the 'Star' Walk had ended, particularly for those members of the Sheffield Race Walking Club formerly Sheffield United Harriers. Almost all their members started with the 'Star' Walk, and we should reflect, in a positive manner, on the impact that the 'Star' Walk has had on the citizens of Sheffield and the wider national and international scene.

This annual event had stood the test of time for almost eighty years beginning with the vision of one or two men who saw Sheffield as being a non-starter for this sport compared with other cities and towns and set out to rectify this.

Their vision has been far better accomplished than they could ever have imagined. A tribute should be paid to them and their succeeding, colleagues who continued to organise the 'Star' Walk long after they had gone.

The first encouragement in maintaining race walking in Sheffield was by the Sheffield United Harriers. Many entrants of the 'Star' Walk immediately joined this club which grew in status as walkers competed against other clubs in the country. Two notable men who maintained a life long interest in and service to the 'Star' Walk, from it's inception were George Grocock, who took part in the first event in 1922 and Jim Hackwood, already one of the few race walkers from Sheffield at that time. Another stalwart was Samson Howard, an administrator with the Amateur Athletic Association. He soon became a race walking judge in the twenties and continued to officiate for many years.

Frank Clay became a leading club member in the thirties. He and Jim Hackwood formed a partnership which kept the Harriers as a leading athletics club by their practical training and methodical administration for many years. Then younger, yet experienced, members took over.

Richard Holland, a leading walker in the fifties also became a judge, rising to officiate at International events. John Eddershaw, who became the new club and event organiser at about 1970, continued until the present date, ably assisted on the coaching side by Jeff Ford who trained novices to be 'Star' Walk winners.

This included three winners of the women's event who went on to represent their country. Also Brian Adams who specialised in training juniors to international standard, continuing the progress of their predecessors Hackwood and Clay.

A special word also for two ladies Pat Hodgkinson, secretary and Helen Elleker, events secretary. Their work was invaluable in the organisation of the' Star' Walk in conjunction with Sheffield Newspapers for whom Peter Gray for several years did all the publicity. He received the applications of entrants, arranged and allocated vest numbers, and liaised with the police and Sheffield Race Walkers until his death in 1993.

At this point in time, the newspaper's proprietors passed over all the responsibility of organising the 'Star' Walk to Sheffield Race Walkers.

John Howley's primary interest was in his daughter Nina's development as a race walker. He never entered the walks but he joined Sheffield Race Walkers and, being ably assisted by his wife Hazel, did all the organising of the 'Star' Walk, which previously had been done by Peter Gray.

John Eddershaw and his colleagues then took over the running of the event on the day itself. Another benefit of the 'Star' Walk was to encourage walking as a healthy life style. Sheffield before the second world war had a smoky atmosphere, with the smoke from house chimneys together with the east end furnaces and steelworks chimneys bellowing out fumes, the air was full with pollution.

The 'Star' Walk having become a traditional event presented a challenge to local men and later women. All started on a level playing field as novices. Many not knowing where this sport would lead them, found themselves not only walking on Penistone Road or Barnsley Road but on the roads of Moscow, Tokio, Oslo or on the athletic tracks of Melbourne.

Altogether over fourteen thousand men and over five thousand five hundred women in twenty three years participated in the 'Star' Walk. Latterly, a further benefit of the 'Star' Walk, was to encourage people's efforts to obtain sponsorship for charities.

Many charities were grateful for money received. Finally the 'Star' Walk had a sociable benefit. When communities almost en masse, would walk along to their nearest point on the course not just to cheer on the walkers but also to meet friends, who some had probably not seen since the previous Whit Tuesday. The 'Star' Walk may pass into folklore but there is a future for young enthusiasts. Juniors have had their own walking races since 1990 and expert coaching has resulted in some of them becoming national champions representing their country as junior race walkers. Training continues today and some will participate in road and track races but alas, they will never have the experience or feel the excitement of being part of the 'Star' Walk.

Dawn White looked quite fresh after her
walk but was she anticipating an
early bedtime?

Carol Wilkinson and Dawn White.

Los Caballeros join
in the fun.

Joanne Wright
leads a group at
Halifax Road.

Two 'ladies' out for a stroll.

No.46 strides out at Hartley Brook

RECORDS
Men 1990 to 2000

Year	1st	2nd	3rd	no in race
1990	Phillip Ward	Frank Wren	John Todd	255
1991	Neil Simpson	Robert Watson	David Lyons	211
1992	Alan Yates	Gary Clarke	Mark O'Farrell	211
1993	Alan Thompson	Mick Masters	Thomas Bidwell	150
1994	Peter Atkin	Jonathan Spiers	Richard Hardy	111
1995	Richard Oldale	Robert Oldale	Mick Masters	75
1996	Robert Oldale	Paul West	Steven White	147
1997	Steven White	Adrian Good	Paul West	86
1998	Nathan Adams	Phillip Hollin	Adrian Good	
1999	Adrian Good	Phillip Hollin	Geoffrey Norton	
2000	Geoffrey Norton	Darren Whittaker	Philip Hollin	

Women 1990 to 2000

Year	1st	2nd	3rd	no in race
	Gilian Watson	Dawne Alinson	Janet Wilson	343
1991	Lorna Lancaster	Cheryl Ellis	Beverley Dunne	229
1992	Lisa Crump	Beverley Cupitt	Gillian Shaw	
1993	Leslie Ashton	Marie Hammond	Julie Askham	135
1994	Nina Howley	Lynn Bradley	Cynthia Lament	124
1995	Lynne Bradley	Beverley Dunne	R. Broomhead	75
1996	Wendy Oldale	Yvonne Bolsover	Beverley Dunne	112
1997	Paula Wilson	Judy Davenport	Claire Tennant	92
1998	Katie Ford	Kerry Laurence	Michelle Thompson	
1999	Tracey Hill	Kerry Laurence	Elizabeth Dunn	
2000	Emma Frost	Georgia Phelan	Karen Macnamarra	

RECORDS
Juniors 1990 to 2000

Year	1st	2nd	3rd
1990 boys 13+	Neil Simpson	Robert Watson	Richard Fauknell
1990 B 11-13	Matthew Rawlings Smith.	Daniel Ward	Matthew Marshall
1990 girls 13+	Lucy Butterley	Marie Walker	Amanda Gould
1990 G 11-13	Nina Howley	Joanne Fitton	Cherry Dawson
1991 boys 13+	Mark Poole	Matthew Rawlings	Alan Chapman
1991 B 11-13	David Massey	Nicholas England	Daniel Rawlings- Smith.
1991 girls 13+	Lisa Crump	Nina Howley	Lucy Butterley
1991 G 11-13	Rachel Burgin	Elizabeth Taranowski	Lucy Ibberson
1992 G 11-13	Alison Tyford	Laura Pritchard	Katie Sneath
1992 G 13-16	Nina Howley	Rachel Burgin	Elizabeth Taranowski
1992 B 11-13	David Massey	Lee Crampton	Michael Brown
1992 B 13-16	Russell Shaw	Jonathan Spiers	Christopher Tune
1993 boys 13+	Jonathan Spiers	David Massey	Russell Shaw
1993 B 11-13	Nathan Adams	Lee Crampton	Steven Marriott
1993 girls 13+	Nina Howley	Sally Tesh	Cherry Dyson
1993 G 11-13	Katie Ford	Katie Bryan	Lynda Hoyland
1994 boys	Nathan Adams	Philip Hollin	Thomas Christian
1994 girls	Katie Ford	Kerry Laurence	Lucy Bishop
1995 boys 13+	Nathan Adams	Philip Hollin	?
1995 B 11-13	Thomas Green	Simeon Adams	Jonathon Brayshaw
1995 girls 13+	Katie Ford	Katie Laurence	Lucy Bishop
1995 G 11-13	Anna Thompson	Dawn Whitaker	Erica Johnson
1996 B 13 +	Nathan Adams	Philip Hollin	Jonathan Laurie
1996 B 11-13	Simeon Adams	Philip Davies	Jonathan Stevens
1996 B u 11	Charlie Patterson	Matthew Heald	Paul Hobson
1996 girls 13+	Katie Ford	Kerry Lawrence	Rachel Carrington
1996 G 11-13	Laura Stepniak	Emma Frost	Leslie Nile
1996 G u 11	Lianne Oldale	Rachel Mersh	Kimberley Shepherd
1997 boys 13+	Nathan Adams	Philip Hollin	Thomas Green
1997 B 11-13	Nicholas Usztan	Ryan Bryan	Jonathan Hill
1997 B u11	Matthew Heald	Samuel Barker	Paul Hobson
1997 girls 13+	Katie Ford	Kerry Lawrence	Emma Frost
1997 G 11-13	Laura Stepniac	Harriet Whiteley	Charlotte Marper
1997 G u11	Rachel Mersh	Lianne Oldale	Rebecca Mersh

Year	1st	2nd	3rd
1998 boys 13 +	Simeon Adams	Ben Holland	Ian Bissatt
1998 B 11-13	Lee Shippam	Branden Brown	K Middleton
1998 B u 11	Samuel Kirk	Chris Spencer	Todd Johnson
1998 girls 13+	Emma Frost	Lisa Taylor	Helen Kean
1998 G 11-13	Lianne Oldale	Sian Ripley	Rebecca Simms
1998 G u 11	Rebecca Marsh	Stefannie Hewitt	Laura Perry
1999 boys 13+	Simeon Adams	Ian Thearsby	Ben Holland
1999 B 11-13	Thomas Fillingham	Chris Pigot	Thomas Kirk
1999 B u 11	Samuel Kirk	Todd Johnson	Christopher Barrett
1999 girls 13+	Emma Frost	Jennifer Frost	Caroline Shaddock
1999 G 11-13	Lianne Oldale	Rebecca Simms	Laura Perry
1999 G u 11	Rebecca Marsh	Steffanie Hewitt	Kelsey Logue.
2000 boys 13+	Daniel Mellor	Mark Paling	S. Own
2000 B 11-13	Todd Johnson	D Paling	D Pass
2000 B u11	M Taylor	J Thornton	T Danford
2000 girls 13+	Lianne Oldale	R Raper	K Shepherd
2000 G 11-13	Laura Perry	Steffanie Hewitt	S Simmonite
2000 G u11	K Eggleshaw	L Eggleshaw	C Caley

Chapter Ten
Star Walk Memories

Audrey is a typical hard working housewife who has brought up four children and as they grew up, she, having more time on her hands, took to working for her local community eventually becoming a local councillor.
Here is her story:-

My Story
By
Audrey Trickett

I completed the "Star" Walk on ten occasions between 1986 and 1998.

I was a member of Sheffield City Council from 1991, also a member of Ecclesfield Parish Council during this time being Chairperson in 1997 and 1998.

The last time that I took part in 1998 the walk organisers gave me the number one. I was very proud of that. Also for the first time every finisher received a medal.

The "Star" Walk was a fantastic way of raising money for charities. The atmosphere was terrific. Families turned out to watch and encourage walkers all along the route cheering us on. Some people would hand pieces of orange or ice lollies to us . Most refreshing!

The earlier walks were nine miles for the women but later we did twelve miles the same as the men.

When I started to feel tired, I just thought of all the money which I was raising for P.A/C.T. at the Children's hospital. Then someone would shout "Come on Audrey" and that would spur me on.

Many people miss the "Star" Walk , it was a great tradition. I am very proud to have been able to take part in it.

Audrey Trickett as she is today (2007) proudly displaying her number '1' card and one of her many certificates.

The term 'Novice' used in connection with the "Star" Walk allowed men to compete who had never previously won a prize in any race walking competition. However, in the nineties this rule was relaxed to allow competitors who had never finished in first place to compete again. This allowed anyone who had never won a prize in any race walking event ,with the exception of junior race walking prizes, to compete again.

Adrian Good took advantage of this rule change and he became the only walker ever to finish in third, second and first place.

Here is his story:-

My Story
A Unique feat
By Adrian Good

It all started in 1988 when I was eight years old. It was a family tradition every year to go down to Hillsborough Park to see the finish of the "Star" Walk. In this particular year, after the race had finished, I walked home with my nan, imitating the walkers. Arriving before the rest of the family and I said to her "One day I will win the "Star" Walk. Sadly two years later nan passed away but I never forgot the promise I made to her.

When I was sixteen years old I entered the "Star" Walk and finished in about eighteenth position but to my astonishment I found that I had won the under eighteen trophy.

I enjoyed the race so much that I spoke to Geoff Ford, the race walking coach, and he invited me to train and learn the proper way to race walk and become quicker.

In 1999 as I crossed the finishing line in first position I thought about my nan and Geoff Ford and I pointed to the skies and said "This one's for you nan". Before I had got my breath back I had news reporters all around me but the first thing was to hug my mum. Then the heavens opened and there was a massive downpour of rain. I thought to myself "Could that have been my nan crying with joy?" It really was the greatest day of my life and I had fulfiled my promise and dream.

I am also the only person to have finished in all first three positions.

My 'Star' Walk Experience
By Ann Lockwood (nee John)

Why did I take part in the 'Star' Walk ?
How could I have been so mad ?
And yet looking back over the years
was it really all that bad?

*Ann Lockwood no 143 poses with her Northern
General Hospital colleagues before the race, and has
a more serious look as she completes the race.*

Setting off from Hillsborough Park,
pounding along Sheffield's streets,
up the hills getting out of breath,
and listening to how the heart beats.

Two years in succession I did it
with my Northern General mates
I've racked my brains and
searched the records
but I can't remember the dates.

It must have been in the eighties
when I was more trim and fit.
Walking then was no problem,
And I didn't mind a bit.

We raised some money for charity
though I can't remember which one
but I do recall the experience
was really a lot of fun.

Another year and more friends before a stern test.

70

My Story
By
Dennis Skinner M.P.
Star Walk Memories

It was April 1956 and an advert in the Sheffield Star for the 'Star' Walk in May, something stirred. I had been a cross country champion and erstwhile marathon runner. Could I succeed at competitive road walking? I decided to try.

The next day I came up the pit at Parkhouse Colliery and started my training. For a whole month I practiced "heel and toe". It was hard work but each day I improved. Soon I was up to nearly seven miles an hour and I sent in an application form. A number was allocated and on May 22nd I travelled by two buses to Sheffield on the morning of the race.

The pace was hectic but after a while I was in second place with only the leader in sight. That's how it finished.- I could have done another twelve miles but I had failed to expand my energy and I regretted not having walked the course before.

In Clay Cross however, it was regarded as a success story. Even my father Tony was proud, which was for him real praise in view of his remarks in the middle of my training when he, like me, a miner came home from the pit and said, " What's this I hear about you walking to Ashover every night waddling your arse".

I protested, "I am training for the 'Star' Walk. Don't be daft , he said, "How can you compete with proper walkers?

My father, a proud NUM delegate, was scared that I was destined to suffer humiliation and was reflecting the views of a Billy Elliot-type parent.

So when I arrived back at Clay Cross with my trophy he beamed.

"Of course I told them at the pit my lad was made of good Skinner stock, of course he'll do well."

My mother Lucy, cast a glance in my direction and it was a look of quiet satisfaction. Unlike Tony, she had never doubted me.

DENNIS SKINNER MP

HOUSE OF COMMONS
LONDON SW1A 0AA

My Story
By
Austin Mitchell M.P.

I remember the 'Star' Walk as one of the great disasters of my short television career. I went down to Sheffield with a Range Rover and a full T V crew to film what was supposed to be a humourous item showing the walk but also getting a bit if fun out of it. Dressed as a walker in full kit (which doesn't quite fit some of my figure) the idea was that I would pretend to be walking and be left behind so disastrously that it would be laughable. Except that it wasn't.

Too many people took my entry seriously so support quickly turned to derision when it emerged how flabby and unfit I actually was.

Sheffield people don't put up with rubbish so easily.

Seeing this was a disaster I gave up. We got back in the Range Rover and filmed the walk for what it was, a competition. At which point in the last section I made the mistake of walking along the side of the leader and eventual winner and interviewed him.

Being pretty whacked by that stage he rightly said nothing and pushed me out of the way.

When I got back to Leeds the producer looked at the film, cut out the last bit and just said 'What an idiot you are'. How right he was. Every time I came to Sheffield in the months afterwards people pulled my leg about it.

My Story
"Sheffield's Mad Walker with the Pram"
by
John Burkhill

In the sixties I worked for Express Dairies and played football for their team.

One of our players did the 'Star' Walk in 1966. He trained hard and said it was a great fitness booster, so the following year three of us formed a team to compete in the 'Star' Walk. However on the day we had to start our milk rounds at three a.m. before we could take part and we just made the start line at High Street in time.

We had trained hard but were no match for the likes of John Warhurst who I think won in record time.

I wanted to become a serious walker and trained hard but did not join the Sheffield United Walkers as family commitments, including my wife being in and out of hospital, was the reason.

I kept competing but the sharp end of the race was too fast for me. Jim Hackwood once gave me a warning for lifting but said, " It's taking part that counts". As the years went by it seemed to me that the 'Star' Walk was losing it's popularity. Crowds which were once tremendous along the route were dwindling. Then came along Sheffield Newspaper publicity manager Mr. Peter Gray who seemed to get the race back on track. He introduced an element of fun but it was still competitive at the sharp end, and his attitude was, "Come and give it a go".

He gave me permission to push my pram around the course collecting for charities. These included Weston Park Hospital, Star Old Folks fund, the Children's Hospital, the Hallamshire Radio Crystal,

John Burkhill with his "charity" pram and a lady marshal at a local marathon. John competed in twenty five annual 'Star' Walks..

the Variety Club, Spring Street Animal Centre and the R.N.L.I. to name just a few.

73

Peter gave me the title "Super John, Sheffield's Mad Walker with the Pram", in one of his commentaries and the name stuck and I am very proud of it.

I have made many friends over the years and received comments which I shall never forget. "Hi ya John, wanna put a motor on for next year", "Tha must be mad, put it on a bus". My favourite spot is Ecclesfield Common where I was offered coffee, biscuits, kit-kats, oranges and from the pub "anything you want". Wonderful people!

So many memories and it makes me feel proud to be a citizen of Sheffield.

Then there was the brilliant organisation and marshalling of the Sheffield Walking Club who always had the safety of every walker in mind. I am so proud and privileged to have known John Eddershaw, John Warhurst, Les Morton and Brenda Lupton as friends.

The way they looked after everyone was first class.

It was indeed a very sad time when the 'Star' Walk finished. I am very proud to have been part of it.

Thanks for the memories, John Burkhill, 67 years young, dated 10 May 2006.

(Editor's Comment. John's daughter died tragically age 29 in 1991. His wife died exactly one year later. John took part in the 'Star' Walk each year 1967 to 2000.)

John Burkhill was given the number 25 recognising his 25th attempt.

Chapter Eleven
Profiles

John Warhurst
The Man with the Golden Touch.

In a race walking career spanning twenty one years, John Warhurst was probably the most popular walker, and of fourteen thousand plus walkers to enter the 'Star' Walk over the years, a dozen went on to gain international honours but John hit the headlines in the Commonwealth Games at Christchurch New Zealand in 1974 when he finished in first position winning the gold medal in the 20 Kilometre event.

He was the only 'Star' Walker ever to win a gold medal in a major event.
His glittering career include the following honours:-

1966   Entered the 'Star' Walk and finished in ninth position.

1967   Entered the 'Star' Walk and finished in first position.

1968   Selected for Great Britain v West Germany, V Czechoslovakia at Stuttgart.

1970   50 Km. Lugano Cup at Eschborn West Germany.

1971   35 Km, G.B. v West Germany at Hillingdon Middlesex

1972   Olympic Games Munich West Germany finished 18th.

       30Km at Milan Italy.

       50Km. G.B. West Germany at Bremen.

1973   20 Km. Lugano Cup semi final in Sweden.

       20 Km Lugano Cup final in Lugano Switzerland.

       10 Km. G.B. v Sweden at Crystal Palace.

       20 Km. G.B. V East Germany at Naunberg.

       20 Km. G.B. V West Germany Warley Birmingham.

       20 Km. G.B. V D.D.R. V Bulgaria Leipzig.

1974   20 miles G.B. V West Germany. At Hamburg.

       20Km.Commonwealth Games Christchurch New Zealand finished 1st.

       20Km. European Championships at Rome Italy finished 9th.

1975   50Km. Lugano Cup semi final in Denmark.

       50Km, Lugano Cup Rouen France, finished 4th.

1977   50 Km. Lugano Cup Milton Keynes.

R.W.A. NATIONAL TITLES

1972   20 MILES. also 50 km.

1975   50 Km.

THE PINNACLE OF SUCCESS. – John's Gold Medal.
From 9th in the1966 'Star' Walk to gold medal winner at the 1974 British Commonwealth Games.

INTER COUNTIES TITLES.

1973 and 1978 Champion.   1975 2nd.

Former British track record holder for 20 miles in 2hrs, 34 minutes; 25 seconds.

SOME OTHER OPEN RACES

John's records include Bradford 50Km winner 6 times, twice 2nd.

London to Brighton 52 miles 1981-3rd; 1982-1st; 1983-2nd.

Manchester to Blackpool 1985 1st.

Isle of man T.T. 1987 1st.

John gives credit to Jim Hackwood and Frank Clay for his development in race walking. As a result of his successes he met some famous people including the then Prime Minister Edward Heath, Prince Phillip, Prince Charles, Princess Anne, Duke of Beaufort, Lord Burleigh, Brian Clough, Kenny Lynch and many others.

In 1992 at The Queen's Garden Party celebrating her fortieth year of her reign, John was invited along with all her international champions plus film and media personalities – A British Who's Who on a special unique occasion.

John – In the words of the Egg-heads presenter on T.V. – Can anyone beat you ? I don't think so. (Ed).

John Warhurst.

John Warhurst Commonwealth gold medallist and world record holder Roland Hardy

PROFILE

John Shepherd

A stalwart who's a credit to golden oldies.

Of the thousands of 'Star' Walkers over the years very few achieve national or international honours. Some take up race walking seriously as a sport and enjoy racing but rarely win a prize for their efforts. Taking part is a joy for them and that is what matters.

One such walker who enjoyed taking part in the 'Star' Walk is John Shepherd. As a young man of twenty one in 1939, he entered the 'Star' Walk and his time was 2hours 19 minutes . In 1987 at the age of sixty nine his time was 2hrs 25 mins only six minutes slower after forty eight years had elapsed. In 1999 when the course had been reduced from twelve to nine miles, at the age of eighty one, by far the oldest competitor, his time was 2 hours 22 minutes.

What a good example of keeping fit to his peers!

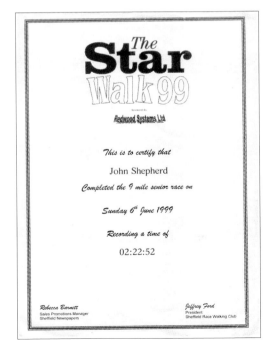

PROFILE

Leslie Morton

Selected seven times for The World's Major Championships.

Comparison has often been made between Sheffield's Commonwealth gold medal winner John Warhurst and Les Morton but whereas the former took part in three major championships, Les took part in no fewer than seven including three World Athletic Championships, two Olympic games and three European Championships, in addition to the World Racing Cup on eight occasions.

His career started in 1983 when he tied with Gary Crossland for first place in the 'Star' Walk. As far as Les was concerned the 'Star' Walk was it and he had no ambitions to go any further. However his coach at the time, Barry Moseley, had included him in the team to compete in the twenty miles Northern race which took part only three days after the 'Star' Walk.

Les says:- "In that race I was walking in a group with John Warhurst and the turning point for me was when I kept catching John's heel and he told me in no uncertain terms to stop it. I decided to up my pace and get away from this group so as not to hinder John any more and not get another telling off.

I came third in that race, not bad for a novice. This inspired me to continue race walking and this is what happened in the following years":-

1984 1st in the Northern 20 miles, 2nd in the National 35 Kms.My first race at 50 K.

1985 1st in 50 Kms.(Luxemburg); 1st Northern 20 miles;1st National 50 Kms; 2nd National 35Kms. Selected for the World Racewalking Cup (I. O. M.)

1986 Set a British record in the Spanish 50Kms. European Championships at Stuttgart.

1987 1st in National 20 Kms.; 1st National 50 Kms.; Broke my toe but was selected for the World Racewalking Cup in New York.

1988 Set a new British record in the Spanish 50 Kms. and consequently selected for The Olympic Games. 2nd National 10 miles.; 1st National 50 Kms.

1989 Selected for the World Racewalking Cup and was first Britain home. 1st National 50Kms.; 1st Burrator 50 Kms with a new British record.

1990 1st National 35Kms.; European Championships in Split Yugoslavia.

1991 1st National 50 Kms.;The World Racewalking Cup in San Jose U.S.A.; the World Athletic Championships in Tokio Japan;

1992 1st National 35Kms. Olympic Games in Barcelona.

1993 1st National 10 miles.; 1st National 50 Kms.; the World Racewalking Cup in Monterrey Mexico; the World Ahletics Championships in Stuttgart.

1994 Les continues " My father was ill with a brain tumour so I helped look after him. He died 6th April which knocked me for six, he used to come with me on my training on his bike around Bradfield and gave me drinks and dry clothing etc., things were never the same. I had been selected for The European Championships but I declined as I couldn't do myself justice. Later that year I won the National 50 Kms at Chesterfield."

1995 Selected for the World Racewalking Cup in Beijing China.; and the World Athletics Championships at Gothenburg. 1st National 50 Kms.

1996 Due to a groin injury didn't race much.

1997 1st Bradford 50 kms.; 1st Dutch 50 Kms international match.;2nd National 50 Kms.; the World Racewalking Cup in Prague contested in a snowstorm.

1998 1st National 20 miles.; 3rd National 10 miles.

1999 the World Racewalking Cup in Mezidon France.

Apart from the incredible record that Les has attained in sixteen years, he has

another string to his bow in that his name is in the Guinness Book of Records for a world record joke race. He along with a friend was dressed as a two-man pantomime camel and ran the fastest ten kilometres in forty four minutes, one second. Follow that!

Who's got the hump

PROFILE

Norman Hopkinson

In 1945 Norman Hopkinson, never having competed in a walking race decided to take part in the 'Star' Walk and after some training finished the course in twelfth position. This was the start of a remarkable career in race walking. He next took part in The Grimesthorpe Feast Walk only a few weeks after the 'Star' Walk and won his first prize as a novice finishing in ninth place.

Two years later after some local races he knew that his best performances were over long distances and consequently entered for the first time in the Bradford Open Walk, a distance of thirty two miles and finished in second position which he repeated another twice and once third in the following three years. In 1950 he was only six seconds behind the winner Harold Whitlock who had been the gold medallist in the nineteen thirty six Olympic Games.

Norman was consistently prolific as a long distance man and competed for this annual event on thirty seven occasions.

The annual Manchester to Blackpool race of fifty two miles attracted him in 1950 and he competed for this race thirty four times.

In 1956, he qualified as a centurion by walking one hundred miles from Sheffield to Harrogate and back and later that year in the Leicester to Skegness one hundred mile endurance race. A centurion is registered by the Race Walking Association as a walker who completes one hundred miles in an authorised race in less than twenty four hours. Including smaller distance races Norman entered over one thousand two hundred races in what is probably the longest career in this sport, lasting over forty years going well into his senior citizenship. He was a truly remarkable man and a resilient one which was a feature of his character. He was also a good club man with Sheffield Race Walkers, always willing to help out particularly at the 'Star' Walk.

He died in 2005 at the age of ninety two.

PROFILE
Betty Sworowski

Entered the 'Star' Walk in 1986 and finished in 1st position.

Holder of U.K. Records :-

2000 metres at Cardiff 2 June 1990 in a time of 8 mins 38 secs.

3000 metres representing England Wrexham 28 7. 90. 12 mins. 49 secs.

Personal Bests :-

5000 metres representing Gt. Britain. L'Hospitalat Spain 6.5.90   21 mins. 50 secs.

10000 metres (National) Redditch. 11.3.89   45 mins. 30 secs.

(This was a U K record but not ratified as the course was found to be 31 metres short).

10000 metres rep. G.B. at Tokyo (finished 20th in the world) 45 mins 59 secs.

15000 metres (National) London 11.5.91 joint first / V Lupton. 1hr. 12 mins. 32 secs.

(This was a new U K record at the time).

Betty represented England or Great Britain at the four major athletic championships :-

Commonwealth Games	Aukland	New Zealand	in 1990.
European Championships	Split	Yogoslavia	in 1990.
World Championships	Tokyo	Japan	in 1991.
Olympic Games	Barcelona	Spain	in 1992.

*Betty Sworowski. No 332
had different patterns of stride
depending on the terrain.*

PROFILE
Helen Elleker

Helen is the daughter of Jack Englert, a local policeman well known in the mid fifties and sixties to travellers through the city centre. Jack directed traffic with his spotless white gloves at the road junction at Fitzalan Square.

Beginning with the 'Star' Walk, Jack was a good race walker himself and no doubt he encouraged Helen to have a go at the 'Star' Walk but he could not have imagined, at the outset, what she was about to achieve.

Helen started race walking in 1980 and trained hard to enter the 'Star' Walk in 1981 which she won. From then onwards she progressed to international level and represented her country on twenty six occasions after special coaching by Jeff Ford.

These are her major achievements :-

National Titles.

10 Kms. Track Championships   1984, 1985 and 1986.

 5 Kms. Track Championships   1986.

10 Kms. Road Championships 1986.

15 Kms. Road Championships 1987.

Personal Best Times.

20 Kms. Road.	1 hour	49 mins	34 secs.	In 1984.	
15 Kms.	1	17	29	1987.	
10 Kms.		47	47	1990	Track. 46.25 in 1990
5 Kms.		23	05	1990.	22.51 1990
3 Kms.		14	11	1989.	13.28 1990

MAJOR CHAMPIONSHIPS

Commonwealth Games   Auckland New Zealand 1990

European Championships   Stuttgart Germany   1986

The World Championships   Tokyo Japan 1991

Also the World race walking cup:-

Isle of Man   1985.

New York   U S A   1987

Barcelona   Spain   1989

San Hose   U S A   1991

Chapter Twelve

Ultra Long Distance Walkers

The 'Star' Walk has always been a challenge for walkers, and as beginners at race walking are classed as novices. They endeavour to master the undulating twelve miles course which, after the comparatively even first three miles, has three steep uphill climbs and three downhill roads to negotiate which tests the most fittest of competitors.

As the race was held at Whitsuntide, the weather was usually hot at mid morning to midday and consequently to finish the course was considered an athletic achievement.

A very few race walkers looking for an even greater challenge took up the gauntlet to participate in the Race Walking Associations longest distance race walks. That is to walk one hundred miles within twenty four hours and thereby receiving the 'centurions' silver medal. In order to complete twenty four hours walking and record the number of miles walked, this race must be competed on the track.

Sheffield has four noteworthy men who started their obsession for this gruelling punishment in the 'Star' Walk. None of them ever won or finished as runners up in the 'Star' Walk but all of them finished their respective walks in the first twelve positions. Norman Hopkinson was an early centurion whose profile is included some pages further on in this book. Jim Hartley was a centurion who finished a hundred miles walking race twice finishing in second position. On one of these occasions the world record was set up by a southerner, Vic Stone, in seventeen hours twenty two minutes.

The third and fourth centurions to note are remarkable in that during their long careers, their achievements are phenomenal and coincidentally both became international athletes but neither represented England.

John Dowling represented Ireland and John Eddershaw-Wales.

Dowling's achievements included nine- one hundred mile races in England which included finishing once in second position at Bristol. However, most of his race walking was done on the continent in open races where he endeavoured to compete five times a year for fifteen years.

He also represented Ireland twice in Sweden and raced for Great Britain at Rouen in France. In other sponsored events he walked from John O' Groats to Lands End and in a six day event at Nottingham he walked four hundred and sixty two miles. The longest ever distance event was a fifteen day one at Hull around a one thousand two hundred metres track covering one thousand miles, John finished it with just twenty minutes to spare. No wonder Prince Charles once said of long distance athletes "They look delightfully demented". Who would disagree with his comment ?

The final member of this quartet is John Eddershaw, once finishing the 'Star' Walk in third place. For over forty years he had a great influence in management matters at the S.U. Club and administration of the 'Star' Walk.

He often commentated using a loud hailer but when the 'Star' Walk lost its original support he said that commentating at that time reminded him of the song " I talk to the trees but they don't listen to me".

Here are the highlights of his career :-

The record of John H.T.Eddershaw

Sheffield United Walkers Club Captain 1969 to 1975

Winner of 12 National Championships and numerous Northern Championships.

1st	Manchester to Blackpool	51.75 miles	1972
1st	Bradford Open Northern	50. kilometers	1975
1st	Northern	20 miles	1975
2nd	London to Brighton	52.5 miles	1975 and 1980

(John's favourite race, competed 20 times)

Qualifed as a centurion, ie 100 miles in 24 hours.

London and Brighton and back   105 miles   1959

Completed 13 100 miles includes one at Rouen France)

3rd	Chigwell	100 miles	1961
3rd	Brighton – Withdean track	24 hours	1981

(Sheffield Record 123 miles 1699 yards)

Welsh A. A. Championships

1st 3000 metres 1975 and 1977

1st 10,000 metres 1975 and 1977

Represented Great Britain on 3 occasions and Wales on 10 occasions

The Centurion's Badge.

Awarded to a race walker who competes in an authorised one hundred miles race and completes the course in less than twenty four hours. Each badge is especially numbered , every succeeding number is given for a new centurion.

THE CAPTAIN'S STORY
John H.T.Eddershaw
3rd Star Walk 1957

The marathon was the one athletic event, in which, in my youth, I wished to compete- but little did I know at the time that it was not to be.

I had watched the Doncaster to Sheffield marathon at Rock House, Conisborough and seen the likes of R.S. Oliver (Reading A.C.) first winner after the war and Olympian Jack Holden (Tipton Harriers A.C.) competing.

Eventually my mother and my three younger brothers moved back to Sheffield in 1951 but it was not until I had completed Army Service that I began to give serious thought to competing at some sport, for I had always been a sportsman.

It was whilst watching Sheffield United F.C. as a regular supporter and watching Brian Richardson who served in the army with yours truly, that I realised that I should be playing with him at football or some other sport.

Eventually, becoming aware of the Star Walk and at the induction of Father Garaway at Rawcliffe near Goole, who was the former vicar of St. Augustine's, Brocco Bank, I decided after consulting my brother Christopher, that the Star Walk would be accomplished before the marathon.

In 1956 I tried to enter the Star Walk on the day, but to no avail.

In 1957 I trained two or three times a week for eight weeks on egg and sherry recommended by Ralph Sharman a gatekeeper at Edgar Allens, Shepcote Lane where I worked. Joyce Clay, a Sheffield beauty queen, who also who worked there, put me in touch with her father Harry who won the Star Walk in 1930 and he advised me to take a longer stride. A complete outsider wearing ordinary walking shoes, I lined up with fifty eight starters on Whit Tuesday June 11th 1957. For the first seven miles Frank Winters and myself were together until the hill up towards Ecclesfield Church where Peter Burrows, the favourite, made his effort. However at Sheffield Lane Top we were more or less together but soon afterwards I began to lose touch. I maintained a good pace until the finish at Corporation Street where amongst the spectators were my mother and brothers Francis and David. They saw me finishing seven seconds behind Peter Burrows.

The crowds that greeted us at the finish were amazing. It was like a Saturday afternoon at Sheffield United or Wednesday football grounds – and we were only novice walkers.

At the reception in Davy's restaurant Fargate, Sheffield United Harriers Race Walking secretary Jim Hackwood invited yours truly to join the club which I did. For the next twenty six years I was to enjoy many satisfactorily experiences of life as a competitor. Finally, the day's excitement took its toll and on arriving back home, I was sick and went straight to bed.

Ultra Long Distance Men

Jim Hartley.

John (Paddy) Dowling

John Eddershaw

Chapter Thirteen

Technique and Training

THE TECHNIQUE OF RACE WALKING

(An article by Brian Adams one time Olympic athlete, now a coach and trainer of young athletes)

Race walking is an event where the distances increase as you move through the age groups with the most common distance being :-

Under 13's (Y 6 &Y7)	2,000 metres
Under 15's (Y8 & Y9)	3,000 m
Under 17's (Y10 & Y11)	5,000 m
Under 20's and seniors	5km, 10km & 20km.

Rules of Race Walking

1. Race walking is a progression of steps so taken that the walker makes contact with the ground so that no visible loss of contact occurs.

2. The advancing leg must be straightened at the knee from the moment of first contact with the ground until the vertical upright position. (There are some races where this rule is relaxed, especially veteran and novice races).

Posture

Keep the body upright, walk tall, don't lean forward- but keep relaxed.

Arms

The arms should be bent at the elbow (90 degrees) with hands brushing past the waist / lower ribs. The arm is like a pendulum and a short pendulum swings faster than a long one, the faster the arms move the faster the legs will move. So don't let the arms drop low. Working the arms hard will drive the legs more like a sprinter than a marathon runner.

Legs

The important thing about the leg action is to ensure that you comply with the rule that requires the leg to be straight from the moment it touches the ground at the front of the stride until it passes through the upright position. Soon after this point the knee will bend to swing forward ready to start the next stride.

Concentrate on:-

Consciously thinking about the knee being straight and that it feels straight. Try walking with a slightly bent knee so that you can feel the difference between a right and wrong technique.

The foot lands firmly on the heel.

Land with the toes pointing up (30 – 40 degree angle), avoid landing flat footed.

Don't plod, to avoid this

Don't overstride as the landing foot will act as a brake, this will develop into a slow plod and the knee will certainly be bent when the foot lands.

Rather aim for a short rapid stride that will keep a good rhythm going.

Get the feet to land in front of each other, i.e. as if landing on a straight line. This produces a smoother walking action.

TRAINING FOR RACE WALKING

The training sessions are similar to those which one could do for cross country running or middle distance running.

Youngsters

Training would obviously depend on age and progress but starting at once or twice a week increasing to three or four times a week in the mid to late teens, a mixture of :-

Race distance	1,000 metres (U11's)	2.000 metres (u13's)
Speed sessions	3 or 4 x 300 metres	3 x 500 metres
Endurance – over distance	1,500 – 2,000 m.	2,500 – 3,000m.

If working with a group, any of the above sessions can be handicapped to make it more interesting and more challenging. Speed sessions can be done as a little relay competition to make it more fun.

Fartlek training is working at different paces throughout a session and can be preset or controlled by the teacher/coach.

Stepping stones – a form of Fartlek is continuous, alternating easy and fast walking or running over 200 metre stretches up to 1,500m or 4,00 metre stretches up to 2,500m.'s.

Walk for three minutes outwards at a good pace, then without a break aim to return inwards before six minutes in total is timed. Progress to four or five minute outwards and back.

Running can also help in training to build up stamina for race walking.

Adults

Longer distance sessions over 10 kilometres or 6 miles plus is for good race walk training, and intervals should be 5 x 1,000metres or 2 x 3,000 metres.

Miscellaneous Pictures

Fun walkers and .....
...a funny Tony Capstick

Happy go lucky George
Hodgson, a wide smile and a
wide stride to match.

Altogether girls – dressed for Judo or walking.

Miscellaneous Pictures

Men's models? Fancy dress ? or 'Star' walkers?

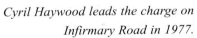
Tony Grocock.

Cyril Haywood leads the charge on Infirmary Road in 1977.

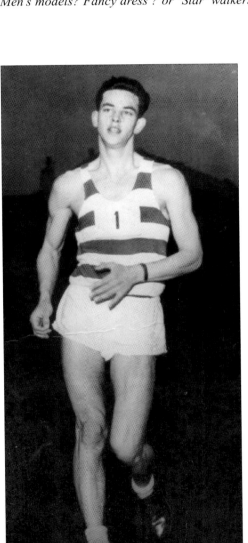

Number one
'Star 'Walk winner Malcolm Tolley.

Miscellaneous Pictures

The start of a 'Star' Walk in the later years – great legs! Note the charity walker with his bucket.

Mr Richard Holland the chief judge looks bemused fearing a stampede as the signal is given for the 'Junior' 'Star' Walk to commence.

Miscellaneous Pictures

The penultimate 'Star' Walk line up in 1999 at Hillsborough Park. How different from starts from Kemsley House in High Street.

All's well that ends well.

Trevor Hibberd and Neil Pearson leading the field at Ecclesfield in 1987.

The Sheffield United Harriers and Athletic Club badge, proudly worn by many athletes and included race walkers for many years.

Chapter Fourteen

'Star' Walk Honours

From 'Star' Walk Novice to International

Major Championships

Star Walk Year	Name	Detail
1947	Lol Allen	EC 1950;OG 1952
1947	John Proctor	EC 1950
1949	Roland Hardy	EC 1950;OG 1952
1949	Albert Johnson	EC 1954;OG 1956 and 1960
1967	John Warhurst	OG 1972;EC 1974;CG 1974
1983	Leslie Morton	EC 1986 /1990;OG 1988/1992;WC 1991/93/95; world cup 1985/87/89/91/93/97/99.

Other Internationals

1956	John Dowling	G.B and Ireland, world cup 1973.
1957	John Eddershaw	G. B. and Wales, world cup 1973.
1962	Malcolm Tolley	G.B.
1973	David Staniforth	England 1977
1974	Mick Greasley	G B world cup team 1977
1995	Richard Oldale	England
1998	Nathan Adams	England (also represented as a junior)

WOMEN

1980	Brenda Lupton	G B world cup team 1983
1981	Helen Elleker	EC 1986;CG 1990;WC 1991 world cup 85,87,89,91.
1986	Betty Sworowski	EC 1990;CG 1990;WC 1991; OG 1992; world cup 1989/91.
1988	Victoria Lupton	OG 1992;WC 1993; EC 1994(also rep. as a junior)
1992	Lisa Crump	G B team world cup 1997

JUNIORS

1968	Jeff Ford	!967;68.
1973	Barry Lines	G B
1985	Susan Ashworth	European Junior Championships 1985
	Ian Ashworth	G B 1985

1988	Zena Lindley	G B 1989
1988	Tracey Devlin	G B 1989/90
1990	Robert Watson	G B 1993
1990	Nina Howley	G B World Junior Championships
1991	Lisa Crump	G B team world cup 1997
1993	Katie Ford	G B
1997	Rebecca Mersh	G B world youth championships

OG – Olympics;   WC-World championships;   EC- European championships;

CG- Commonwealth games

ADDENDUM

Quips and Quotes

The Pilot

On person who was always "in the lead" in The 'Star' Walk was not in fact a walker at all but the pilot.

Before the days when a motor car carrying a loud speaker or a computerised time indicator on it's roof rack, the pilot went before the walkers on a bicycle.

The crowd always cheered him as they knew it was imminent that the first walkers would be on the scene.

A familiar face for many years on the bicycle was Harry Cooke, a native of Ecclesfield who himself had a keen interest in race walking as he had competed in The 'Star' Walk finishing second in 1946.

The pilot's role was simply one of necessity in order to comply with the rules because walkers just had to follow the crowd lined streets to find their way to the finishing line, and in case race stewards were in attendance at cross roads and other road junctions.

Harry Cooke of Ecclesfield was second in the1946 'Star' Walk but thereafter led for many years on his 'bike' as the pilot before a motor car was used carrying a computerised clock which enabled the leader and spectators to check the times en route.

Quote from The Lord Mayor. Alderman J H Bingham 1954.

"Walking is the finest exercise. It requires no apparatus, the stage was always prepared, it was one of the two greatest exercises to which the body and mind could be put", The other he said was gardening.

FOR READERS WHO HAVE COMPETED IN THE 'STAR' WALK.

SELF CERTIFICATION

THE ANNUAL 'STAR' WALK

Competitor.........................

Year   . . . .

Distance   . . miles

Time   . . hours . . , . . minutes

Finishing position   . . .

Number in race   . . .